KAIRÓS

ALSO AVAILABLE FROM BLOOMSBURY

The Bloomsbury Italian Philosophy Reader
edited by Michael Lewis and David Rose
Law and Chance by Emanuele Severino
Beyond Language by Emanuele Severino

KAIRÓS

In Defence of 'Due Time'

GIACOMO MARRAMAO

Translated by
Philip Larrey and Silvia Cattaneo

BLOOMSBURY ACADEMIC
LONDON • NEW YORK • OXFORD • NEW DELHI • SYDNEY

BLOOMSBURY ACADEMIC
Bloomsbury Publishing Plc
50 Bedford Square, London, WC1B 3DP, UK
1385 Broadway, New York, NY 10018, USA
29 Earlsfort Terrace, Dublin 2, Ireland

BLOOMSBURY, BLOOMSBURY ACADEMIC and the Diana logo
are trademarks of Bloomsbury Publishing Plc

First published in 2022 in Italian as *Kairós: Apologia del Tempo Debito*

First published in Great Britain 2024

Cover design: Ben Anslow
Cover image: Kairos, Caeros from the Hermitage Museum
(Contributor: Grigur, Own work, CC BY-SA 4.0, Wikimedia Commons)

A catalogue record for this book is available from the British Library.

ISBN: HB: 978-1-3504-3117-1
PB: 978-1-3504-3118-8
ePDF: 978-1-3504-3119-5
eBook: 978-1-3504-3120-1

Typeset by RefineCatch Limited, Bungay, Suffolk
Printed and bound in Great Britain

To find out more about our authors and books visit www.bloomsbury.
com and sign up for our newsletters.

To Gabri

forever

The time is out of joint; – O cursed spite,

that ever I was born to set it right!

William Shakespeare, *Hamlet, I,* v

CONTENTS

PREFACE TO THE ENGLISH EDITION (2024)

My now forty years of philosophical reflection on the question of time is punctuated by a trilogy consisting of three books: *Power and Secularization: The Categories of Time*; *Minima temporalia: Time, Space, Experience;* and, finally, *Kairós: Towards an Ontology of Due Time*.

Power and Secularization (*Potere e secolarizzazione* 1983; new expanded edition 2005; translated into German, Spanish and Portuguese) represented a decisive turning point in my intellectual itinerary. With this book, the philosophical problematic of time comes to occupy a neuralgic position. Time, in an axial relationship with the question of power, will from then on come to constitute the core of my reflection. In the perspective I outlined, the 'theorem of secularization' offered the most effective analytical pattern for reconstructing the genealogy of power: starting from the 'long wave' represented by the rupture produced in the body of Western civilization with the irruption of the symbolic constellation of linear time of the Judeo-Christian matrix. A cumulative, irreversible and future-oriented temporality thus broke the paradigmatic and synoptic circularity of the Greek conception of time, making the prophetic word the first form of disenchantment of the world and historical time the trajectory of a progressive secularization of *éschaton*. In line with Max Weber and Karl Löwith – and in spite of Heidegger and his 'history of nihilism and metaphysics' – both Athens and Jerusalem encapsulate the destinal cipher of the West. The metaphorical and symbolic constellation of the 'infuturating' time (with the pillars constituted by the ideas of Progress, Revolution, Liberation) was thus delineated as the inescapable reference horizon of the modern concept of universal history or 'world-history' (*Welt-Geschichte*) which, beginning with Kant, was destined to permeate the entire vicissitude of the philosophy of history between the nineteenth and twentieth centuries. In reconstructing the stages of Western rationalism from the perspective of the metamorphoses that had invested the intuition and experience of time, the book called into question philosophic, artistic and literary references. It dealt with the Schmitt-Blumenberg controversy around secularization, with the 'history of concepts' (*Begriffsgeschichte*) of Otto Brunner, Werner Conze and Reinhart Koselleck, and with not only German, as in the case of Hans Blumenberg's complex work, but also research in the Anglophone world on metaphorology, starting with Hayden White's seminal *Metahistory*. But it included in its trajectory the very story of the natural and social sciences: from the first scientific revolution to the epistemological turn represented by Niklas Luhmann's systemic paradigm and René Thom's catastrophe theory. Moving against the tide of philosophical postmodernism, to which it contrasted the category of *hypermodernity* (understood in a sense not far removed from the term *surmodernité* adopted a few years later by my dear friend Marc Augé), the book took its starting point from Ludwig Wittgenstein's thesis that the cumulative and 'infuturative' temporality of progress is not a mere character of the Modern, but on the contrary constitutes its *form*: a 'typically constructive' (*typisch aufbauend*) form, whose activity consists in erecting 'an increasingly complex structure.' From this premise, I had come – through a philosophical reconversion of Koselleck's 'semantics of historical times' – to the conclusion that the *hypermodern* experience of time, punctuated by an ever more intense and dizzying acceleration of innovations, was represented by the syndrome of the 'past future': of a future no longer expected or intended as a hope for change but experienced as *déjà-vu* and repetition-reminiscence of the identical. All of this goes to show that the motif of 'acceleration', before it was discussed more recently as *novissimum* by sociologists like Hartmut Rosa,[1] was as well present since the 1970s–1980s in Koselleck's conceptual genealogy as in the philosophical reconversion I made in works on secularization and the experience of time. In a later volume, *Heaven and Earth* (*Cielo e terra* 1994; translated into German and French), I traced the long series of semantic shifts and metaphorical extensions through which the lemma 'secularization' – whose horizon is represented by a typical Western dualism the eternity/secular pair – has been transformed from a *terminus technicus* that originally arose in the legal sphere into a theological and philosophy of history notion, until finally denoting the crisis of any model of 'oriented history': in a hypermodern climate bounded at the two poles by the disenchantment operated by science and the overbearing return of the myth of Origin that characterizes both the various forms of religious fundamentalism and the 'invention of tradition' that presides over the formation of *imagined communities* (as the title of a famous book by Benedict Anderson sounds). While the theses of *Power and Secularization* became *the* subject of intense international discussions (particularly in Italy, Germany, France and Spanish- and Portuguese-speaking countries), a *stricto sensu* theoretical deepening of the question of time was being carried out by me in two subsequent works, *Minima temporalia* (1990–2005–2022; translated into German and Spanish) and *Kairós*.

In these works, which somewhat anticipated the themes of the *spatial turn*, I was operating a 'lateral shift' of the viewpoint adopted in my genealogical research on secularization. In controversy with the conceptions of Bergson and Heidegger, who postulated – with, admittedly, very different declinations – a pure or 'authentic' form of temporality, more original than its representations/spatializations, I argued for the inseparability of the time-space nexus and, referring to contemporary post-relativistic physics, traced the structure of time to an aporetic and impure profile, with respect to which the dimension of space constitutes the inescapable formal reference for thinking its paradoxes. The philosophical alternative I advanced was thus coming to be outlined – through a cross-comparison with the languages of art and science – as a *post-metaphysical ontology of difference*, conceived in open rupture with the current declinations of the theme of nihilism. Unlike postmodernism, it was no longer played out on the usual surpassings and reversals, but on a 'perspectival deangulation': on a radical displacement of the optics with which the entire Western philosophical tradition – from Plato to Bergson, from Aristotle to Leibniz, from Nietzsche to Foucault, from Baudelaire to Benjamin – has so far visualized the question of time. A decisive strategic role has since come to be played in my work by the category of *difference*. This category, derived from a confrontation with the variegated archipelago of feminist philosophical thought that began since the 1970s (I am thinking particularly of the pioneering work of Carla Lonzi, Luce Irigaray and Luisa Muraro), is taken up as a reconstructive criterion of a non-identitarian universal (understood not only in plural but also in inherently conflicting terms) in my more recent works: from *The Passage West* (2012; also translated into Spanish) to *The Passion of the Present* (2008; translated into Spanish) and *Against Power: For an Overhaul of Critical Theory* (2016). In these works, a welding is made between the genealogical and theoretical perspectives, represented by

Minima temporalia and *Kairós*, in order to shed light on the conceptual and symbolic constellation of our global present.

But a further moment of clarification is necessary. The perspective of a *universalism of difference*, already outlined in the first Italian edition (2003) of *The Passage West*, is resumed and developed in *La passione del presente* (2008): a work orchestrated in a series of keywords intended to serve as a possible lexicon to circumnavigate, moving from different conceptual locations, the logic and structure of our world-modernity. A famous sentence by Hegel assigned to philosophy the task of understanding its own time in thought. This specifically philosophical responsibility, characteristic of the modern age, is not, in my view, devolvable to other knowledge, much less surrenderable to those who proclaim themselves repositories of the resources of meaning. But the prospects of an ontology of the present cannot be confused – as is the case, for example, with Foucault – with an 'ontology of actuality'. In order to think radically about the present and bring it to the concept, it is necessary to be able to grasp that secret inactual (*untimely*: not turned to the past but, in the Nietzschean sense, anticipatory) fold that bears within itself, as Kant puts it, the *signum prognostikon* of a future, of an *ad-veniens* understood not as a 'horizon' but as a symbolic 'energy' capable of producing an opening of experience toward the future. This explains the meaning of the title: whereby 'passion of the present' – of a present, then, that challenges us – is meant not only the involvement of philosophical reflection in the destiny of its own time, but also the way in which philosophical subjectivity itself, as indeed every other subjectivity, is implicated by the present in suffering its burden and necessitating logics. The programmatic assumption of the book explicitly posed the need to make the two poles represented by the different philosophical styles of analytics and hermeneutics interact. Keeping the field of tension between these two traditions of thought open imposes itself as an unavoidable condition not only to come to terms with the dilemma between 'truth' and 'interpretation' that currently paralyzes contemporary philosophical research, but also and above all to weld the diagnosis of the present to the dimension of possibility and decision, orienting it toward the perspective of an ontology of the contingent and the Event. This task appears all the more urgent in the face of a global conjuncture increasingly marked, on the symbolic level, by the implosion of the future (and the dominance of the 'past future') and, on the theoretical level, by the widening of the gap between absolutism and relativism. The thesis underlying the book thus moves from the influential scene of a world-modernity marked by the transition from the 'colonization of the future' (operated by the Western ideology of progress) to the 'eternalization of the present': a present whose *imago aeternitatis*, marked by the paradoxical coupling of agitation and sterility, feverish acceleration and stagnation, risks expunging from the horizon the 'kairological' dimension of conjuncture, and thus of the possible and the contingent. The identity violence that characterizes, under the guise of religious fundamentalisms, the (transterritorial and transcultural) conflicts of a glo-calized world, at once unified and diasporic, is nothing but the interface of an age of 'sad passions', induced by the crisis of the future as a horizon of expectation. And yet, alongside the perverse intertwining of these phenomena of depressive implosion and molecular explosion, traceable to the pathogenetic aspects that the logic of identity tends to assume, we see emerging in different areas of the planet liberating pushes that demand a multilateral reconstruction of the universalist project: moving from the realization that – to paraphrase Hamlet's famous warning to Horatio – there are more forms of rationality (and, consequently, more paths to freedom and democracy) than our poor philosophy has hitherto been able to imagine. To such a reconstruction pointed, on the philosophical level, the plot woven by the key-words of the book: in the conviction that only from a radical critique of substantiveist and reified notions of the Self, and from the acquisition of the irreducibly dynamic-processual, at once relational and antinomian nature of all identity (whether personal or collective, cultural or religious), can the theoretical-practical perspective of a *universalism of difference* hinged – according to a fruitful Kantian intuition – on the logic of 'disjunctive synthesis' be opened.

It will now fall to me, in conclusion, to set up three different scenes in quick summary, in order to clarify the relationship that the works that make up my trilogy on the question of time establish with each other within this path.

The scene of *Power and Secularization*: a temporality that, in a tortured affair of ruptures and recurrences, emancipates itself from the cyclical model to give rise to an increasingly accelerated and infuturing linear time that, even in its secular versions, continues to bear within itself the traces of messianic promise.

The scene of *Kairós*: the irruption, at the mysterious suture point between 'line' and 'circle,' succession and recursiveness, of the qualitative time of decision.

The middle scene of *Minima temporalia*: space as a presupposition of both the everyday experience of time and the enigmatic and alienating aspect of cosmic time.

Picking up these books of mine again, I find it difficult to escape the impression that I have come to the same conclusions as some theoretical physicists, but following a diametrically opposite trajectory. While the latter, starting from the spacetime of relativity and quantum gravity, have arrived at the Augustinian (and, in some cases, even Heideggerian) identification of time with 'ourselves,' my itinerary, traced along the borderline between philosophy, science and art – from the 'Augustinian despair' over the familiar inexplicability of time to the Renaissance perspective, from Heidegger's 'perspectivist constitution of being' to

Baudelaire's 'death of time' and 'lived space' – made a drastic lateral shift from the philosophical *refrain* of the antithesis between the authentic time of 'inner duration' and the inauthentic time of spatialization. The fruitfully 'visionary' character of physical science has always been intertwined with the flashing insights of art and poetry. And scientific revolutions, punctuated by deadly executions of previous images of the world, have had an impact not only on the practices of science but on the dizzying ruptures that have marked the vicissitudes of philosophical conceptuality itself.

It happened thus following the first scientific revolution, Galilean and Newtonian: with the traumatic unravelling of the *deception of the senses*, which had led us to believe in an immobile Earth at the centre of the solar system.

And it is happening today with the new picture of the universe unveiled by general relativity and quantum physics: with the squaring of the *deception of the arrow of time*. But the stakes of this deception directly affect us: our lives and our place in the universe.

In the new worldview, the 'Now' and the 'Here' have lost their universal meaning, to be reduced to mere 'indicals'. Time and space lose their absoluteness, marking the checkmate of all 'presentism'. Space is not a container but is curved by bodies. And with it, time also curves. Matter is energy, but energy is not a *continuum*: it is discontinuous, composed of quanta, and varies like light. The vibrations of the gravitational field do not spread through space: they *are* space. Reality is not an aggregate of entities but a dynamic of relations. It is not Substance but Event. And yet the aim of quantum gravity theory is to delineate an *imago mundi* that excludes the concept of time from its horizon. So wrote the physicist Carlo Rovelli a few years ago in an essay with the programmatic title, *Forget time*:

> Following a line of research that I have developed for several years, I argue that the best strategy for understanding quantum gravity is to build a picture of the physical world where the notion of time plays no role at all. I summarize here this point of view, explaining why I think that in a fundamental description of nature we must 'forget time', and how this can be done in the classical and in the quantum theory. The idea is to develop a formalism that treats dependent and independent variables on the same footing. In short, I propose to interpret mechanics as a theory of relations between variables, rather than the theory of the evolution of variables in time.[2]

Indeed, neither Einstein's relativity nor the quantum and elementary particle physics of Schrödinger, Heisenberg and Dirac admit a unidirectional sequence of time from past to future. The order of that strange thing we call time is itself symmetrical: it arranges past and future as *simul ante retroque prospicientes*. The arrow of time, according to Clausius (who introduced the concept of entropy), is given only when there is heat transmission. The drive into the future depends on the low entropy of the past: since heat cannot pass from a cold body to a hot one. But this would seem to happen only in a clipping or subset of the universe that gave rise to time, living organisms and our existences.

Time succession would therefore be a 'deviant' syntax from the 'elementary grammar' of a timeless world, which (as McTaggart had argued back in 1908) contemplates no distinction between cause and effect but only 'regularity'.

Coming to a conclusion in this regard is a line from Ludwig Wittgenstein in a letter to John Maynard Keynes dated 3 January 1913: 'I forgive your insults to Philosophy, considering that you had just seen McTaggart and were thinking of me . . .'

Whatever one thinks of McTaggart's old thesis and the new theses of quantum gravity theorists on the unreality of time, the fact remains that, in the low-entropy cutout of this holographic universe in which we happen to live, every mark, every fold, every curve of our bodies is, in the words of Paul Valéry, 'a parameter of time'.

And the only way for us humans to live is to grasp the event of *kairós*. That 'due time', *qualitative time* of decision making that is radically other than the numerical neutrality of *chrónos*, of mere chronological succession incapable of conveying the 'signs of the times': the *sēmeia tōn kairōn* of which Matthew's Gospel speaks (Mt., 16:3).

Many questions remain, in all evidence, open.

But, as a great artist-philosopher – and magnificent Nobel laureate – of my generation said, 'the answer is blowin' in the wind . . .'

G.M.

Rome, August 2023

PREFACE TO THE NEW ITALIAN EDITION (2020)

In his famous allegorical personification, Lysippus depicts Kairós as a winged child in the act of resting his left foot on a sphere. On the left, the flexed leg supports the body, and the arm holds a razor on which the scales oscillate. On the right, the leg is extended to compensate for the mass. While part of the weight is still on the outstretched wings, the muscular contraction betrays the effort to maintain a precarious balance before taking off again.[1]

According to the sources, the prototype of the allegory – destined to give rise to various versions, in the form of marble reliefs or gems, during the subsequent centuries – would have been created in Pella, for Alexander the Great, between 336 and 334 B.C.E. It is likely that Lysippus produced the fortunate allegory in several specimens. But what is certain is that, with the spread of the Lysippean image, the concept of *kairós* will acquire an ever wider range of symbolic connotations, capable of encompassing all the previous meanings: the 'right point' for a mortal wound, as already in Homer; the 'suitable time', as in Pittacus; *power and effectiveness*, combined with the criteria of 'harmony' and 'measure', as in Gorgias; the 'virginal' character, associated by the Pythagoreans to the virtues of the number 7 (influential scene from which directly descends the anthropological figuration of Kairós as an adolescent shy of any possession); and finally – last, but not least – the critical, decisive and fruitful moment.[2]

The feminine personification of Kairós with the *Occasio* in the sphere of Latin culture inaugurates a figurative proliferation as suggestive as it is misleading with respect to the symbolic and semantic density of the 'kairological' constellation. Suddenly, we find ourselves in the presence of a case of translation-betrayal so striking as to go almost unnoticed. The translation into *Occasio* – which in its 'feminization' nevertheless maintains attributes similar to those of the Lysippean youth – certainly appears to be underpinned by a fertile intuition: the intuition of a secret affinity between the Greek *kairós* and the Latin *tempus*. But – this is the point – it declines exclusively in the sense of *caducitas*: of a timeliness aimed at facing the inexorable acceleration of a Time *edax rerum*, 'devourer' of all things, a time that irremovably *fugit* (flees). To seize the moment, the propitious moment, is an act that coincides with the appearance of a virtue directly born from the need to face the vortex of the destroyer Time, which involves everything in a perpetual 'fury of vanishing': a virtue with a hybrid appearance, as it can only be a *carpe diem* melancholically declined in a post-Christian key.

Hence the welding between the figures of Chance and 'Father Time' which – as Erwin Panofsky documented in a memorable essay[3] – pervades, under the name of *Fortuna*, the protomodern symbolism of great Renaissance art. This includes, and rightfully so, that political art which has its brilliant inventor in an author (Renaissance by definition, once all harmonizing stereotypes of the Renaissance have been dismissed) such as Niccolò Machiavelli: nothing illustrates better the flavor of the era than Machiavelli's conception of the image of Time which, in a famous Medici tapestry, 'grabs Occasio by the hair'. However, this is a profound alteration of classical symbolism: since the child-Kairós, youngest son of Zeus, unlike the woman-Fortune cannot be caught from behind (having the bald nape of the neck) but must be 'faced' and taken by the forelock that protrudes from his forehead. And yet.

And yet, precisely for the reason just mentioned, the extraordinary fame conquered in the modern age by the figures of *Occasio* and *Fortuna* has gone hand in hand with a progressive oblivion or loss of the symbolic density enclosed in the concept of *kairós*: a density accessible only on condition – as I propose in this book – of radically rethinking the equation of *kairós* and *tempus*, starting from a perspectival deangulation able to take us back to the enigmatic origin of the Latin lemma.

But what is there to discover in such a familiar and obvious term as *tempus*? In reality, whoever asks such a question does not realize that inexplicability is often nothing more than the implication of obviousness, and that sometimes right behind the most familiar words of our lexicon lie the most disturbing (but also most fruitful) paradoxes of our experience. Few have thought about the fact that the word 'time', derived from the Latin *tempus*, encompasses in itself in Romance languages the two terms that in English and German indicate, respectively, chronological time and meteorological time: time and weather, *Zeit* and *Wetter*. Now, curiously enough, the etymology of this lemma is extremely uncertain. For a long time it was thought to be a noun deriving from two Greek verbs: *teino*, which means to stretch, to extend, to strain; and *témno*, which means to cut. Both hypotheses would seem, in fact, to recall plausible senses: the image of time as stretching or *continuous* and that of time as a break, rhythm, *discontinuity*. It happens, however, that this double etymology is – also because of its intrinsically dilemmatic structure (the hypotheses of continuous and discontinuous have, as is known, constituted a paradigmatic antithesis in the history of philosophical and scientific thought of the West) – largely unsatisfactory.

Investigating the mystery of the origin of the Latin *tempus*, I came across an essay by Émile Benveniste, in which I seemed to glimpse a possible key to a solution. It is good to keep in mind that this key was proposed back in 1940, but almost never taken into consideration by philosophers: with the unique significant exception of my late friend and teacher Michel Serres, with whom I have had the opportunity to exchange views on several occasions.[4] Benveniste's thesis sounds roughly as follows: the difficulty in discovering the etymology of *tempus* derives from the fact that the compounds of this term are actually older than the word 'time' and therefore bear much more archaic traces of the noun itself. The noun *tempus* is therefore born from the abstraction of lemmas such as *tempestas, temperare, temperatura, temperatio*, etc. The word *tempus* – I observe in the book – signals, almost surprisingly, the wisdom inscribed in the genetic code of a language capable of consecrating a single word for two phenomena that we have come to consider distant or even heterogeneous. It is as if the uniqueness of the term carried within itself the awareness that what we call 'time' is nothing more than a point of intersection between different elements, from which the evolutionary reality originates: a 'mixture' ('to cut' does not perhaps also have the meaning of 'time'?) that makes *tempus* something very close to what the Greeks *called kairós:* the *right time*, the *opportune time*.

Referring back to these reflections of mine, and referring explicitly to the thesis I put forward in this book, a great linguist and romance philologist like Harald Weinrich pointed out – in the context of a wide-ranging reflection on the 'Hippocratic scissors of time', centered on the *incipit* of the first aphorism of Hippocrates: *Ho bios brachys, he de techne makre* (i.e. *vita brevis, ars longa*) – the need for a radical rethinking of the whole issue, advancing a further, suggestive proposal: the traceability of the origins of tempus to the 'pulsological' dimension of the times (*tempora*), as the appropriate location for measuring the speed of pulsations. In this way – in a sense entirely complementary to that implied by my thesis – the dimension of time would coincide with rhythm: along a line of convergence between medical art and the poetic and musical arts.[5]

In this context, Weinrich observes, 'it is possible to revisit *ex novo* the question, highly controversial and debated among lexicographers, of the etymology of terms central to culture such as *tempus, time,* and *Zeit.* Is it really plausible, one wonders, to affirm that a Latin word such as *tempus* is related to the Greek verb *témnein*, 'to treat'?'. And, accurately quoting a passage from *Kairós*, he adds: 'On the unclear etymology of the word *tempus* Giacomo Marramao writes: 'It is necessary to go back to thinking about language by examining [...] the mystery of the origins of the Latin *tempus*.'[6]

The implications of the thesis appear at this point disruptive even from a strictly philosophical point of view: the Greek equivalent of *Tempus* is not *Chrónos*, but *Kairós*. Clearly differing from other etymological hypotheses, in fact, Benveniste had associated the term *kairós*, deriving from the Indo-European root *krr-, to the meaning of the verb *keránnymi*, 'to mix', 'to temper' (where 'temperance' is at this point not only that of climate, but also that of rhythm), reaching the conclusion that '*tempus* coincides, in its different meanings, with *kairós*'.[7] Far from meaning 'instantaneous moment' or 'occasion' – according to the 'Renaissance' reception mentioned above – *kairós* thus comes to designate, like *tempus*, a stratified and extremely complex figure of temporality: a figure that refers to the 'quality of the chord' and of the opportune mixture of different elements – exactly like atmospheric time. In its spatial version, on the other hand, the same lemma has indicated – since Homer – the 'proper places', the vital parts of an organism 'in form', that is, balanced, tempered and rhythmic in its components.

My genealogical investigation ended, therefore, with the statement of a thesis and – at the same time – with the formulation of an idea: perhaps the very idea of *tempus-kairós*, taken in its *double profile of instant of the timely decision and due time of the 'temperance' and of 'the proper mixture'* as an event that interrupts the continuum and as a fruitful tension between different energies and powers, is able to give us back the sense of our evolutionary cut-out and, with it, of the grammar of our forms of life.[8]

It is from here that I would now like to compare the 'kairological' constellation with the phenomenology of our present: a present in which the existence of each of us seems to be ensnared not only (as postulated by Paul Virilio) by the 'dromomania', by the imperative of speed, or (as postulated by Reinhart Koselleck) by the *acceleration* imprinted by the domain of global Technology, but more specifically by the syndrome of haste.[9] And it is because of this syndrome, which goes hand in hand with the simultaneously securitarian and emergency status of a topicality dominated by the return of the anxiety/politics pair and the consequent political use of fear, that the experience of time today appears dangerously close to how it appeared to Hamlet: *out of joint*, off-axis with respect to the questions of meaning and purpose that invest the dimensions of our singular existence as well as our being-in-common.

My emphasis on the need for a philosophical reflection on time and its paradoxes should not mislead. It does not mean at all that the concept of time is the exclusive prerogative of philosophers, while scientists would be responsible only for 'measuring' it and poets only for 'feeling' it. On the contrary (and I imagine that this phrase will disappoint many), in spite of the fact that philosophy has been racking its brains for 2,500 years on that enigmatic and perturbing *familiar stranger* called 'time', *there is no time of philosophers*. There are – Einstein stated poignantly – only two times: *psychological time* and *physical time*. Each one of us experiences time on a daily basis: it therefore has a range of variations as potentially wide as our subjective sensations. The second one is not only relative to the reference systems of the different observers but – and this is the other, decisive face of Einstein's relativity – it has instead an objective limit, a general physical constant independent (according to Maxwell's equations) from any parameter. This limit, this constant, are represented, as it is known, by an insurmountable numerical barrier: 300,000 km/sec of the speed of light. Beyond that barrier, the speech about before and after has no more sense. Photons, particles travelling at the speed of light, do not 'have time', do not age. Those who superficially mistake Einstein's revolution for a form of 'relativism' have not considered – or simply ignore – that this consequence of the principle of relativity is the determining aspect of the whole theory: in nature no signal – and, consequently, no body – can move at a speed higher than the speed of light.

I do not intend to dwell further on this point. But it will be opportune to keep it well in mind in the background, because it marks a 'perturbing', a cosmological disorientation, which is the horizon of the current existence of all of us: inhabitants of a universe that, if it has no longer been that of Ptolemy for almost five centuries (to be exact, since 1543: the year in which Copernicus, shortly before his death, published the *De revolutionibus orbium cælestium*), is now not even that of Galileo and Newton.

From here, I would like to articulate my introductory considerations on three levels, which I will explain in an extremely brief and schematic way:

(a) first, the *feeling*, or *internal sense*, of time;

(b) secondly, the *temporal syndrome*, which refers directly to the 'spiritual situation' of our present:

haste.

(c) thirdly, the practical-normative side of the question: that is, what to do.

The solution (wary of considering it as a recipe or a 'therapy') that I put forward refers, as we have seen, to an image of Kairós not as a mere *Occasio* but as the 'due time' of the encounter between arrow and target, inspiration and work. The 'kairological' time appears therefore, in my perspective, as the only possible point of intersection between project and existential reality, or – in a broader sense – as a potential angle of convergence between two temporal dimensions that today appear dramatically divided and conflicting: 'time of life' and 'time of the world', or – going down in scale – 'private time' and 'public time'. I will return to this aspect at the end. But, in the meantime, let us turn to the first two points.

Feeling of time, internal sense of time – we said. The experience that each of us has of time depends on a number of factors. Stimuli, first of all. The presence or absence of stimuli produces a decisive variation in the way we experience time. The same period, so to speak objectively, of time, time measured by the calendar or the clock, may appear full or empty depending on the number and intensity of the stimuli, of the stimuli to which we are subjected. Hence the paradox pointed out by Kafka: when we have 'all the time', i.e. an empty and indistinct time, at our disposal (as, for example, in certain periods of long pause between one work commitment and another or during a vacation period), just then we realize that we 'have no more time'. So it happens to us, the inhabitants of the hypermodern condition, to live intensely only in the interstices of an 'all full' time. This is already a first and very important indication of the syndrome of lack of time.

Second factor: age. We know from a series of empirical studies carried out in Western countries that time is perceived as longer by young people, less long instead or tending to be shorter (with proper exceptions, of course) by older people. For those who are older, time seems to pass more quickly.

Third factor: anxiety, the stress coefficient. Anyone who lives in a global city, in one of the great metropolitans of the planet, already knows from having experienced it first-hand – and without having read Simmel's pioneering essays on the subject – that stress leads to a different estimate, a different perception of the same amount of time. The sixty minutes of an hour spent in a state of work or psychological stress give us a feeling of 'duration' different from the same hour spent in a state of well-being or relaxation.

Finally – last, but not least – we have the factor of gender difference: the famous 'women's time'. In women, vital time appears to be structured and ordered according to a different scale of priorities than in men. Surveys carried out in various countries of the industrialized West show how women declare themselves to be normally (apart from the inevitable exceptions) tied to an order of factors (space assigned to affection, to the sphere of intimacy, to the demands of family life, etc.) that often appears dissymmetrical with respect to the agenda of their male companion, whose time schedule is mostly perceived as cumbersome or inconvenient.

This quick list of factors should suggest the need to characterize in a circumstantial way, under the historical-cultural profile as well as under the structural one, the root of the *temporal syndrome,* warning us against too easy generalizations. The 'pathological' aspects are not to be trivially traced back – in peace with today's rehabilitators of Bergsonism – to the mere discrepancy between the internal and external sense of time, to the inevitable hiatus between measured time and inner time: for the simple but decisive reason that that hiatus signals an existential gap found, in different forms and degrees, in all ages and in all cultures. The *syndrome of haste,* in other words, although to a certain extent innate to the '*condition humaine*', which makes us projecting animals, naturally technical, naturally artificial animals, is something intimately connected with the modern (as it has been for the last two centuries, starting from the era of the industrial revolution) and hypermodern (typical, that is, of the dizzying technological innovation of the last thirty-forty years) experience of time.

Therefore, haste – not speed – contains within itself the code of the 'spiritual situation' of our time. This is a decisive distinction. The temporal syndrome that marks the hypermodern condition is not speed as such. The Greek world greatly valued speed, which was considered a factor of virtue: it is not for nothing that the Iliad praises Achilles in his prerogative of 'fast foot' (*podas okus*). However, speed was virtuous only insofar as it was functional to the purpose: only to the extent that it proved effective, capable of achieving the objective. The dimension of haste, of the precipitation of time, had no place in Greek culture: haste, senseless and 'imprudent' acceleration, misses the target just as much as slowness, hesitant delay. Haste and phlegm, precipitation and hesitation, are but two specular forms of untimeliness. The classical model, therefore, remains linked – as in the Lysippean symbolism – to the 'virtuous' tension of opposites from which the temporal decision is generated: a tension to which speed and prudence, readiness and conformity to the purpose contribute in equal measure.

Haste is something else. It is the separation of speed from purpose, of means from end. It is the self-mindedness of speed *sans phrase*, of innovation as such, of *Novum*: of the 'new' as an end in itself.

But what is the source of this syndrome of haste, which seems to characterize all the manifestations of an era that I have long preferred to call *hypermodern* rather than postmodern? It derives, as I have tried to highlight in a series of investigations started in the seventies and then merged in my already mentioned book, *Potere e secolarizzazione*, from a pathogenetic factor: the autonomy of the modern Project of Enlightenment matrix (in its twofold progressive and revolutionary aspect) from the aims and objectives that originally limited it, relating it to the concrete pragmatics of specific subjects and contexts of experience. Technical-scientific rationality – or, to quote Jürgen Habermas, 'instrumental reason' – thus becomes self-validated and released from the purposes that had constituted it. With the transition from the industrialist phase to today's post-industrial society, technological innovation takes on a predominant role, imparting a dizzying acceleration to all productive, distributive and communicative sectors of associated life. From a means of implementation of purposes defined, the project ends up transforming itself into a technical acceleration of change and – according to the poignant expression of Octavio Paz – 'colonization of the future'. The pathology that is produced at this point is given by a *hypertrophy of expectation*, which is matched by a *progressive narrowing of the space of experience*. The widening of the horizon of expectation corresponds to a reduction in the margins of experience. The inflation of expectations is matched by a deflation of experiential capacity. The projecting 'protention' of expectation swallows up experience, transforming the future into *déjà-vu*. The future no longer appears, as it did at the time of the industrial revolution, to be a free dimension, but an innovative routine removed from the will of individuals and delegated to impersonal technological structures, ranging from corporations to the great complexities of global communication. Time is no longer 'available', within our reach, but rather appears to us as an *a priori* dimension removed from our ability to decide. It is as if we moderns had built a 'future-centric' society in which the future, instead of being available as a solution to our vital problems, had imploded, folding into the *past future*. This has produced that syndrome of the modern condition that was foreseen, with extraordinary anticipatory ability, by Shakespeare, when he placed in Hamlet's mouth that beautiful and shocking phrase that you will find *in exergo* to this book: *Time is out of joint,* it has gone off its hinges: 'Damned fate', continued poor Hamlet, 'to have been born to set it right'. Like Hamlet, we too live a life off-axis with respect to the time we live. Constantly leaning toward the future. Or reclining toward the past. But still unable to 'hinge' on the present. Unable to take the decision that alone allows us to 'put time back on track'.

The syndrome intuited by Shakespeare is only apparently disproved by those psychological investigations that find one of the most characteristic pathologies of contemporary society in 'presentism': in an obsessive concentration on the present, which renders some individuals (especially young people, but not only . . .) incapable of planning for the future as well as re-elaborating the past. The present eternalized in the neurotic fixation is in fact, in this case, the same present that eludes decision-making. The return to the present cannot be done mechanically. The mentally ill appear locked in the actuality of the present: powerless to make sense of the world and their actions in the world. As Husserl, Jaspers and Binswanger had observed, it is proper for the mentally ill to remain trapped in pure *præsentatio,* without any retentive or protentive capacity.

Schematizing to the extreme, we can say that there are two ways of reacting to the contemporary temporal pathology. The first way is given by the melancholic syndrome, typical of those who feel captured by a retentive depression and devoid of 'dream planning': it is typical of the depressed person that feeling of fatality that translates into the impression of always arriving 'too late' to the appointment with life. The second way is given instead by the manic syndrome of those who, crushed on the present, always repeat the same gestures, the same scene. An attitude that descends directly from an interdiction to experience the past: from an inability to mourn that gives rise to the constant repetition of the same neurotic scene. We can therefore conclude on this point by saying that the 'bad' eternity of the present works exactly according to the Freudian mechanism of removal and compulsion to repeat.

And then: *What to do?* What way out of the temporal pathology? It is certainly not up to me to propose therapies: the exercise of philosophy – unlike what some of my zealous colleagues think – is not aimed at curing souls, but at understanding things. Serious therapists, on the other hand, know very well that no subject can be effectively cured if his resistance to self-knowledge and to the realization of his real conception are not removed. Therefore, let us first try to understand the structural and conjunctural profiles of the realities in which we happen to live. We all know, by now, that 'Western rationalism' (the *Okzidentaler Rationalismus,* as Max Weber called it) has long since crossed the borders of Europe and of North America itself, extending to the entire planet. Beginning with the symbolic date of 1989 (the year of the fall of the Berlin Wall), this expansionary process is increasingly being labeled 'globalization'. Of course, not all the phenomena that are presented today as new by those who they talk about the 'end of history' are really so: we have been talking about globalization since the 18th century, about a 'global age' since the years of the First World War. And yet today the process seems to assume an intensity of scale previously unknown, by virtue of the welding between market logic and post-electronic or digital technologies of 'real time'. The economic-financial and multimedia synchronization of the different areas of the planet seems to have transformed what was once the modern experience (limited to the elite of the industrial countries) into Modernity-world. But the structure of modernity-world is by no means linear, let alone homogeneous. That same process of globalization of markets and technologies, which on the one hand is homogenizing, on the other induces new phenomena of localization and cultural differentiation. Far from being a legacy of the past and of tradition, the 'local' (with the search for identity, the return of the community, the 'invention of tradition' that characterize it) appears today to be intimately inter-connected with the 'global' in a sort of biunivocal and, so to speak, interfacial relationship. The phenomenon of the 'glo-cal', of the short-circuit of global and local – of which some sociologists speak today and of which I have proposed a substantial redefinition in my work – was foreseen by the great prophet of our 'techno-tronic' era, Marshall McLuhan, when, in his diagnosis-prognosis, he characterized the 'global village' as marked by an ambivalent dynamic: of planetary unification and 'tribal decentralization'. It is not by chance that today we have a return of interest in comparative studies, not only geopolitical, but above all geo-economic and geo-cultural. And it is not by chance that the international discussion finds one of its gravitational centers in the theme of Asian values, demonstrating that it is precisely the nature of globalization that activates the need for a differentiated analysis of the different areas of the world market. One need only think, for example, of the way in which an Anglo-Indian economist such as Amartya Sen has updated and corrected Weber's comparative survey, observing that the economic miracle of the 'tigers of the Pacific' (South Korea, Singapore, Taiwan and, in geometric progression, China itself) can be explained only by the prevalence of forms of practical conduct marked not by an individualistic ethic (as in the West), but rather by a collective ethic with a religious base founded on the sacrifice of the individual to the community purpose (be it that of the family, the corporation or the State).

Understanding the globalized world therefore also means understanding the dynamics of differentiation and re-localization of identity that it induces with the new forms of planetary conflict.[10] Understanding the symbolic complex that underlies the two faces of globalization is an indispensable condition for operating effectively not only in the cultural and political sphere but also on the economic and financial level. But this understanding also includes a corollary that is difficult to avoid: the need for a self-recognition of the West through the comparison with the other great cultures of the planet. Today, not only does the fate of Europe as a *global player* caught between the 'great spaces' represented by the United States and China depend on this ability to self-reflect, but also the future of the guiding principles of the West: from the value of the person to the notion of human rights. Modern Western civilization, the place of origin of the syndrome of haste, must prove itself capable – by accepting the challenge of cultural otherness – of acquiring a politics of the possible and the contingent intertwined with an ethics of finitude. It must learn to positively decline the limit, seeing in it not an obstacle or a lack, but on the contrary an opportunity: a condition to give meaning to our experience, to our concrete forms of life, reconquering the future not as a guaranteed and undifferentiated progress, as 'homogeneous and empty time' (W. Benjamin), but as a contingent dimension and as an opening of the horizon of possibilities.

Only in this way will we be able to see in the apparently indecipherable complexity and conflicts of the present not a threatening factor but the key to accessing the extraordinary richness of a plural world, without vertices and stable centers, marked by an irreducible multiplicity of experiences, images and 'narratives'. Only in this way we will succeed in recomposing within ourselves the temporal multiverse that permeates the grammar of life forms: time for work and time for love, time lost and time gained. This is the dimension of time that I call 'kairological': the only one able to reconnect, in a fruitful tension, past and future within the present of experience and creative imagination.

A Greek dimension, as I was saying. But, in the end, not very far from the concept of time that we find expressed in a great biblical text such as the book of *Ecclesiastes:* there is a time to be born and a time to die; a time to weep and a time to laugh; a time to mourn and a time to rejoice; a time to be silent and a time to speak; a time to hate and a time to love; a time for war and a time for peace.

Recapturing the sense of this plurality and this tension means keeping in mind, simultaneously, both sides of the Kairós: the cut, the decisiveness of the decision, and the shrewd perception of the 'due time', of the propitious conjuncture. It means, in other words, regaining – as heirs to the ruins of the Modern – a 'timeliness' without hesitation and without haste capable of triggering a fruitful interaction between the dimensions of universal and singular existence.

In the perspective of a planetary being-in-common.

POSTSCRIPTUM

This work is presented in an expanded form (enriched by the new preface). The text of the first edition, published by Laterza in 1992 and remained unchanged until the third edition of 2005, is presented here only with some formal changes and few bibliographical additions.

I had initially thought to integrate the theme of the book with two additions: one dedicated to the treatment of Kairós in the Hebrew theological tradition (with a development of the research I had carried out in my previous works on time and secularization); the other was destined to the comparison between 'presentism' and 'eternalism' and to a deepening of the philosophical implications – or rather of the feedback on the philosophical conceptuality – of the way in which the scientific investigation has come in the last two decades to touch the 'wall of time'. But the volume of the collected notes had now grown to such an extent that it increasingly took on the structure of a new book, which I hope to publish as soon as possible.

In the meantime, it would be a good idea to keep in mind the multiple dimensions of temporality: 'an idea of punctual time, almost a subjective absolute'; a 'time determined by the will, in which the future is as irrevocable as the past'; and finally 'a multiple and ramified time in which each present bifurcates into two futures', giving rise to 'a growing and dizzying network of divergent, converging and parallel times'.

What could be better than Borges' dizzying essay on time, *El jardín de los senderos que se bifurcan*, mentioned by Italo Calvino in *Molteplicità*, the last of his *Lezioni americane*, conceived 'for the next millennium'?

Kairós ideally forms – together with *Potere e secolarizzazione* and *Minima temporalia* – a philosophical trilogy on time that aims to indicate, along the shadow line between theoretical and practical philosophy, a possible way out of the syndrome of the 'past future' (and of what, with a suggestive Spinozian formula, has been called the age of 'sad passions').

The preface partly takes up the Prólogo *to the Spanish edition*: *Kairós. Apología del tiempo oportuno*, translated by Helena Aguilà, Gedísa, Barcelona-Buenos Aires-México 2008.

This new edition is dedicated to the memory of Michel Serres.

G.M.

Florence-Rome, May 2020

FOREWORD

Familiarly foreign, mysteriously obvious, time lies at the crossroads between daily experience and its representation. At the center of philosophical reflection since its inception, the temporal dimension permeates each moment of our lives. Yet, it is very difficult to produce communicable knowledge about it. Thus, our discussions on time seem inexorably constrained by the words we use to convey an ineffable *feel of time*.

According to a *leitmotif* of twentieth century philosophy (from Bergson, to Husserl and Heidegger), our experience of time would be marked by a profound and invisible wound: the juxtaposition between a 'proper' time – authentic but incommunicable, which expresses the subjective and inner sense of *duration* – and an 'improper' time –inauthentic but measurable, that manifests itself through its objective and spatialized representation. On the other hand, a specific 'pathogenesis' of temporality is typical of the modern experience. It derives from the disparity between the wealth of possibilities opened to individuals by the technical-scientific project of the control of nature (and of rationalization of social evolutionary processes) and the poverty of its experience. From this derives a phenomenon of *acceleration* (genealogically traceable to the Judeo-Christian roots of Modernity), for which time splits up between an endless projection towards the future, and an atrophy and fossilization of the past, which progressively deprives the present of the space of its existence. The *temporal bifurcation* that is created between experience and expectation, between the finite nature of time and the infinity of desire, also describes the impossible correspondence between individual life and the temporal course of the world. On the one hand, indeed, the temporal course of the world precedes and outlives individual life, thus proving the inevitability of the split between existence and project. On the other hand, 'asynchronies' inevitably rise within Historical Time, times and rhythms that change according to the fields and domains of action.

These are the *philosophical* diagnoses of the 'temporal disease'. But are we certain that philosophy has given a decisive contribution to the framing of the question of time?

The core argument of this book is that this century's philosophy – precisely in its would-be most radical formulations – has relinquished its original function, by neutralizing those *paradoxes* of the nature of time that, conversely, science has taken as both the premise and the condition of its work. The aim of the reflection proposed here, however, is not limited to describing the constant elements (or the innumerable metamorphoses) of the modern and post-modern 'visions' of time; neither is it to 'reinstate' – *sic et simpliciter* – the neglected dimension of space. Its aim is an attempt at identifying the dimension, that is, the *space*, of 'our' *time*, starting from the *cosmic disorientation* that the new scientific image of the universe has transmitted to our experience.

There was only one way of pursuing this goal: to establish a link between 'Plato's world' –or, better, the Platonic 'shifting of gaze' – and the 'perturbation' that is implicit in the *space-time* of Einstein's relativity and in the *indeterminacy* of quantum mechanics. However, this entailed a difficult decision: to distance ourselves from that line of philosophical reflection –which is fundamentally 'familiarizing' and 'anthropocentric'– that, starting with Aristotle, then through Augustine, Bergson, Husserl and Heidegger, touched on the cosmologies of the *arrow of time* themselves.

At the end of this journey, the image of *Kairós* will emerge: it is no longer the Chance or the Fortune of the Moderns, neither is it the eschatological event of the Christians; rather, it is the fundamental dimension of the appropriate time, of the *crucial moment* that is nothing but that part of each 'identity', within which the very phenomenon of the mind, or Awareness, *takes place*. The *Kairós* will enter the scene with a *coup de théâtre*, as indeed is appropriate for this representation of time. At that point, with a surprising move, its destiny will intertwine with another aspect, which is also both decisive and neglected by professional philosophers: the mystery of the origins of the Latin word *tempus*.

This book is based on a cycle of lectures I gave at the Istituto Italiano per gli Studi Filosofici di Napoli in December 1990 (I will never be grateful enough to my friends Gerardo Marotta and Antonio Gargano for creating a place of encounter and reflection that has been rarely replicated on the international philosophical scene). Other important and enlightening moments of verification for the arguments presented here included: the Römerberggespräche held in Frankfurt, in June 1991, devoted to the 'question of time', where I presented the essay *Die Grenzen der Zeit*; a cycle of lectures and conferences that I gave last year in Spain (particularly at the Universities of Madrid, Barcelona and Murcia); a discussion with Tullio Regge on 'The Problem of Time in Physics and Philosophy', held in Naples within the 1991 edition of 'Futuro remoto'; a seminar on my previous volume *Minima temporalia*, organized and then published by the journal of psychoanalysis *Koinos*, Vol. XII (1991), No. 1 (edited by Gianni Nebbiosi, with essays by Francesco Corrao, David Meghnagi and Lucio Russo).

The present work is linked to my two other books on the question of time (*Potere e secolarizzazione. Le categorie del tempo*, Rome: Editori Riuniti, 1985; *Minima Temporalia. Tempo, spazio, esperienza*, Milan: Il Saggiatore, 1990), with which it ideally forms a 'triptych'. Compared with the preceding publications, however, this book further develops the discussion, rather than simply deepening it. As recalled above, its subject is not only the deconstruction-reconstruction of the classical, modern and post-modern notions of time, towards a hermeneutic-critical analysis of the side-effects inherent to the 'temporalization' of historical *prágmata* (*Power and Secularization*); neither is it to move the focus of the investigation from time to space, towards a philosophy of experience (*Minima Temporalia*).

The aim of this book is, rather, to identify the constitutive *residue* of 'our' time – starting from the contemporary and 'disorientating' spatial-temporal dimension and far from any pretence of 'authenticity'.

The format is that of one long *lecture*, in which expository and analytical-conceptual parts alternate and – this is my hope, at least – complement each other.

For this reason, footnotes were reduced to a minimum; they also privilege classical authors and primary sources, at the inevitable expense of secondary literature.

G.M.

Rome, June 1992

Common abbreviations were used for references to ancient classics. As for Greek words, we sometimes preferred to disregard the scientific transliteration criteria (Editor's note).

1

A ghost of space

The coin of time also has another side. This adage is not new, even if, as such, it was vigorously voiced by the most radical expressions of twentieth-century philosophy, from Henri Bergson to Husserl and Heidegger. While diverse, these reflections shared a common tone: to rescue time from the tyranny of *Chronos*, to oppose the *authentic* time of 'inner duration' to the *inauthentic nature* of measured time. There could be no better reverse side to Newton's operation; for him, 'to rescue time' meant to take, as *absolute duration,* the chronological flow – the only one which was knowable because numerable.

But the two sides of a coin are not simply juxtaposed. Rather than representing an antithesis, they form an invisible network of reciprocal implications and references. This is what I will try to show by drawing directly – as much as possible – from some key works. It is not necessary to belong to the 'hermeneutic *koiné*' to know that the interpretative layers that, in the 'course of time', have come to rest on these texts affect us also subconsciously.

They act on us independently from our will or awareness. The relinquishment of the illusion of a 'direct grasp' of reality represents – as one will see – the *leit motif* of my discussion. To re-propose it for some, perhaps very classic, works would then be the symptom of a worrisome naïveté, in addition to being self-contradictory. This, however, does not detract from the fact that, in the *topical moments* of Western history, some decisive turns were due precisely to the 'return' to the vitality of some classics, finally freed from the surcharge of tradition or – to use a more elegant expression – relieved from the hermeneutic redundancy and the scholastic deformations of the *vulgata*. Let us verify from texts, then, up to what point we can legitimately assume the paradigmatic juxtaposition between the 'two sides' of time, from the philosophical – that is, rigorously *conceptual* – point of view.

The coordinates of Newton's definition of time are, in reality, more complex than what the philosophers of 'temporality' would have us believe. Indeed, in the *Principia* (*Philosophiae naturalis principia matematica*, 1687), Newton does not speak of *one* time – unlike Gassendi; rather, he speaks of a splitting of time into 'absolute' and 'relative', 'real' and 'apparent', 'mathematical' and 'vernacular':

> Absolute, real, mathematical time flows uniformly, in itself and by its very nature, with no relation to anything external; with another name, it is called *duration*. Relative, apparent

> and vernacular time is a sensible and external measure of duration through motion that (be that right or wrong) is commonly used in lieu of *real time*: such are the hour, day, month and year. [...] Possibly, no motion is so uniform that we can accurately measure time by means of it. All motions can be accelerated or delayed, but the *flow of absolute time* cannot be changed. The duration or the persistence of things remains the same, whether the motions are accelerated, delayed or cancelled; for this reason, and rightly so, this duration is differentiated from the sensible measures; this is done through the astronomical equation.[1]

In order to grasp the meaning of this very famous and literally epoch-making excerpt, it is necessary not to miss or misunderstand the radical distinctions that it establishes. The first distinction is explicit, and clearly separates the uniform flow of absolute time from the markings of relative time, whose 'vulgarity' consists in its dependency on sensible daily experience. The second is an implicit but no less decisive distinction between *measure* and *number*. While measurement falls within the category of vernacular time, because it is obtained through a reference to the external element of motion, the Number represents the measure of invariance of that absolute time, whose duration is real as much as it is *mathematical*, hence free from the mistakes and tricks of the senses.

It is truly superfluous to insist on the relevance of these definitions, which will affect all subsequent disputes on time and space, up to the formulation of relativity theory:

> Newton's absolute time and space – notes J. T. Fraser, founder of the International Society for the Study of Time – connected by the relation $v = d/t$ (speed = distance/time), permitted a scientific vision of motion that gave our understanding of nature a unity higher than that of Copernicus' heliocentric universe. After Newton, there were no longer privileged celestial bodies; the physical laws of motion could be extended to all the bits of matter that moved in the universe. There was no need to refer to the sun, and even less to earth. This wider vision allowed Newton to formulate the first truly general principle, the universal law of gravity.[2]

Keeping this background firmly in mind, I will limit myself to mentioning another aspect, which is essential to the development of my discussion.

The drastic sketchiness of some stereotypes, of the constructs transmitted by the *vulgata*, negatively weighs on Newton – as on the majority of great authors. The most famous of these constructs insists – as is well-known – on the categorical nature of the pair absolute space/absolute time. From the *scholium generale* at the end of the *Principia*, it would indeed seem that the enduring character of the pair space/time has its conclusive onto-theological foundation in a metaphysics of the divine Presence. I say it *would seem,* because Newton correctly avoids identifying God with time and space. To the contrary, He constitutes their *foundation*: God 'is not eternity or infinity but is eternal and infinite; he is not duration and space, but lasts and is present. He always lasts and is present everywhere and, while existing always and everywhere, He *grounds* duration and space'.[3] A very delicate and subtle question is raised here, which will constitute the backdrop of some key moments of the dispute between Leibniz and Clarke: the question related to the famous *sensorium* metaphor.

An important fact, even if often ignored, is that Newton uses the expression *sensorium Dei* only for the definition of space, *not* for the definition of time. It would seem legitimate, then, to deduce that time cannot be intended as a divine *sensorium* on a par with space. Things thus standing, it would seem legitimate to also conclude that, given Newton's definitional premises, the question of the ontological nature of time – the 'what is it?' – substantially remains unanswered. Stated otherwise: how are Divine presence and temporal Duration comparable, if God is unchangeable and eternal, while Time 'flows'? Of course it may flow uniformly, but how can it still be true that it *flows*?

Hence – it is worth remembering, even if only briefly – Leibniz' objection to Newton: the statement 'time flows' cannot be taken as a 'principle', nor can it be taken as a logically necessary 'postulate'.

It is, rather, a statement of fact. In fact, it is a *factum brutum* of which nothing meaningful can be said, given that it eschews any logical justification. In order to make this fact 'intelligible' we must make that necessary transition 'from mathematics to physics',[4] which forces us to refer to another principle: the *principium reddendae rationis,* or principle of sufficient reason (for which *nihil est sine ratione*: nothing happens without a reason for which it happens this way and not in any other way).[5] Following this reasoning – as we know – Leibniz reaches a double rebuttal. On the one hand, he rejects the notion of 'absolute space', whose autonomous existence, when considering the void as the limitation of divine freedom, would contradict the *principium reddendae rationis.* On the other hand, he rejects the idea of 'absolute time' and of uniform duration, in favor of a notion of time as 'the order of sequential existences'. Within this notion, 'moments, outside things, are nothing', because 'they consist of nothing but their sequential order; and, this remaining unaltered, one of the two conditions, for example the presumed anticipation, would differ in nothing from the other [condition] that now exists, and could not be distinguished from it'.[6]

If we analyze Bergson's concept of 'actual duration', in light of what we just mentioned, we find a complete inversion of the Newtonian idea of 'absolute time'. Bergson – like Newton – uses the terms 'duration' and 'flow' to define real, authentic time. However, he uses the same words for the exactly opposite meaning: he does not intend to refer to the homogeneous and empty time-quantity of physics – essentially reduced to a 'ghost of space' – but to the time-quality of 'psychological existence', of interior awareness[7] – as we can already read in his *Essai sur les données immédiates de la conscience* (1889). The novelty of Bergon's position, then, does not simply consist in the vindication of the rights of finitude, of the 'relative' time of our daily perception and experience of things, even if that element of Jewish anxiety for which – as Bergson's student Vladimir Jankélévitch noted – 'for the first time in the history of doctrines 'mobility' does not express the unhappy condition of creatures'; in fact, 'sadness turns into joy when creatures, once they stop seeing themselves as exiled in the midst of Heraclitus' becoming, recognize, in change, their very homeland and substance', is far from negligible in the philosopher's works. The true novelty of Bergson's thought lies in the affirmation of the *incommensurability* of time and space, of internal duration and external world,[8] in terms so radical as to produce its unilateral as much as its paradoxical character, its inconsistencies as much as its 'deletions'.

2

Plato's cinematography

Yet, as we mentioned at the beginning of this work, the theme of the *uni-duality* of Time – that is, of its ancipital nature – is not new. For millennia, Western thought has believed to see, within the relationship that *daily experience* maintains with the dimension of time, a peculiar phenomenon of *bisection*. This phenomenon has been described in many ways. It is, however, possible to define it – with an inevitable simplification – as 'a qualitative difference between *lived time* and the *concept of time*'.[1] Or – maybe more appropriately – it is possible to render it with the following expression: a *sense* or, if one prefers, a *feel* of time corresponds to the *representation* of time. In the latter, time is necessarily externalized and spatialized, while, in the former, it is seized in its 'authenticity' and 'purity': a vital flow, 'qualitative multiplicity with no resemblance to the number'; 'organic development, that is not a growing quantity'; 'pure heterogeneity, within which there are no distinct qualities'.[2]

In order to render this phenomenon of bifurcation, classic Greek employed a double definition of 'time' as *chronos* and *aión*. But what is the correct meaning of these words, of these two 'names of time'?

Clearly, the first refers to the quantitative and homogeneous dimension of 'chronological' *sequence*, while the second refers to the qualitative and incommensurable dimension of *duration*. Yet, things are much more complicated than what a linear distinction such as this might have us believe. We will try to explain the reason of this statement in the simplest and most schematic way.

First of all, for Greek thought – unlike the twentieth century philosophies of time – the two dimensions of time should be understood as complementary, rather than as antithetical.

Second, the articulations of time that we are dealing with – time as 'chronos' and time as 'aión' – encompass a set of meanings that have progressively been lost in subsequent translations and simplifications.

Yet, both aspects – *complementarity* and *polymorphism* – are fundamental, if we want to grasp some of the developments of the reflection on time as were carried out by the two greatest philosophers of ancient times: Plato and Aristotle.

Let us take, as an example, an excerpt from Plato's *Timeus*: the famous passage 37d, which contains the *first complete definition of 'time' in Western philosophy*. According to the *vulgata*, time is defined here as 'the moving image of eternity'. This is the common interpretation, which we can find in many philosophical works and which was taken up by Borges in his extraordinary *Historia de la eternidad.* We are facing here one of those instances in which the translation does not do justice to the wealth of implications of the original text. As a matter of fact, Plato's definition calls forth both names of time that we recalled above, while linking them in an intimate relation: *chronos* is the moving image of *aión*.

In what sense, 'image'? Is it in the sense of imitation, imperfect 'duplicate'? In such a case, the time-*chronos* would indicate an example of the logical fallacy of the 'simulacrum',[3] which would be consistent with the usual criteria of a rigidly dualist interpretation of Platonism. But, if this interpretation were correct, Plato would have used a specific word to express the term 'image': *eídolon*. He used instead another word: *eikón*. The definition, then, starts to acquire its complete form: *chronos* is the moving icon of *aión*.[4] In the fullness of its formulation, the definition also acquires another appearance, a meaning different from that suggested in its *translation*, which, in reality, was its *betrayal*: *chronos* is not rejection and abandonment; it is not the 'fall' into the *aión*, precisely because it is not pure *eídolon*, simulacrum, but rather *eikona*, authentic image of eternal *duration*. The 'chronological' and the 'aionic' moment, therefore, are neither antithetical nor exclusive. Hence – as Simone Weil had perceived, contrary to many professional philosophers, and as her student Simone Pétrement documented – they do not engender any 'dualism' in Plato; rather, they belong to each other within a single model.

But there is more. What are the implications, on the ways we understand our experience of time, of saying that *chronos* is the necessary and 'moving' (*kinetón*) image (*eikona*) of *aión*? In order to answer this question – which already brings us to the Aristotelian concept of time – we need to examine all the meanings included in that semantic pair (and which seem to have been ignored by great part of the modern and contemporary reflection on the question of time).

Chronos is a word that, certainly, indicates *measured time*, what we commonly mean by the expression 'chronological time': the time marked by a clock. Its Greek meaning, however, is both more complex and comprehensive, and more correctly refers to the expression *numbered time*. *Numbered* and *measured* are two different things. Plato was well aware of it when he specified – in the same excerpt from the *Timeus* that we quoted – that *chronos* is the *moving* image of *aión* because it proceeds 'according to the number' (*kat'arithmòn*).

If *chronos* cannot be reduced to the flat homogeneity of measurement, to empty 'exteriority' but, rather, relates to the *number* (a dimension that, in Aristotle, will directly call forth the *soul*), *aión*, on the other hand, is not limited to a static and indifferent 'eternity', but rather refers to the image of *vitality*, intended as the energy, or *virtue, of lasting*.

Postmodern philosophers and scientists, that today proclaim the 'end of eternity', and the detachment from the 'a-temporal model' of classical physics and metaphysics, should seriously reflect on the richness of these excerpts. The original meaning of *aión* is 'vital force', as evidenced by its approximation to *psyché*.[5] In Homer, therefore, the term still holds a human connotation, and equals individual life: Patroclus dies because the *aión* in him has been killed (T 27: *ek d'aión péphatai*).[6] On the other hand – as already documented by Benveniste in 1937 – the neutral terms *ayu* and *ayus* 'indicate, in Vedic, the 'vital force' as individual [. . .] or universal [. . .] principle, capable of identifying with life itself [. . .] or with its duration'.[7] In the same essay, the root **aiw-* is connected to **yu* and **yuwen-* and, as a consequence, to the Indo-European forms in -en- (such as *yuvan* in Sanskrit and *iuvenis* in Latin) that have specialized to express the vital energy of youth[8]. This would allow us to shed light on some tacit implications of the Greek symbolism of time, with the simple help of etymological-linguistic analysis. Inside this symbolism, indeed, Aión is commonly represented as a young man or a boy, while Chronos almost always appears as an old man. The idea of the regenerative moment implied in the association of **aiw-* and **yuven-* seems to be also reflected in the Latin expressions for 'eternity'. The Latin correlative of *aión* is, indeed, *aevum*. Originally, however, this word, that conveyed the *animated* and *vital* image of duration, was masculine, *aevus*, and did not have a plural form. It is indeed not a coincidence that both *aetas* and *aeternitas* (that is linked to the Greek adverbs *aién*, *aèi*, 'always', and to the Germanic *ewig*, which itself derives from the Gothic *aiws*) are the Latin derivatives of *aevus*, *-um*. *Aión* implies, therefore, a representation of time based on the biological metaphor of growth: 'aionic' temporality can only be understood as an organic form, as a *characteristic weave*, or *organism*, endowed with its own persistence and endogenous cycle, and capable of self-regenerating (*autozoon*).

This said, a question of a more philosophical character still remains unanswered. This is the question that André-Jean Festugière[9] lucidly posed in an important essay of 1949: how has such a diametrical inversion of the relationship between *aión* and *chronos* been produced? Through which steps – and semantic skids – could it happen that that which originally indicated the vital individual duration in opposition to absolute chronological time ended up representing the latter's horizon, even posing itself as *tou chronou patér*?[10] The answer given by this hermeticism and classical culture scholar lay in locating the turning point of the philosophical history of the word in Empedocles' fragment 16.[11] Here, the *aión*, used in reference to the *sphairos*, would denote an individual life that lasts indefinitely. It is precisely in this sense, of *infinite individual duration*, that *aión* would be made to refer to the living-model in the *Timeus*.[12] During the past centuries, this theme – as is well known – has engendered numerous disputes, producing great divergence and interpretive polarizations that have continued even to this day. In light of our analysis of Plato's text, however, neither the 'durational', nor the 'non-durational' interpretations prove convincing, where the first understands the *aión* as infinite time, 'endless life',[13] while the second understands it as an 'aoristic punctuality that excludes past and present, while being reduced to the "is"'.[14] Both interpretations seem in fact to miss a fundamental point: the link between the two dimensions of Time; what we could call the 'interfacial' connection that is established between *chronos* and *aión* by means of the Number.

The recourse to the *arithmós* has a fundamental consequence on the relationship between the 'two sides' of time: the *crisis* (in a literal sense) of 'aionic' time, the introduction of a *caesura* in the flow of duration. It is difficult to say whether the etymological deduction having *chronos* derive from the same root as *krinein* – which means 'to divide', 'to separate' – is simply suggestive or sound. At the same time, both the Greek noun *krisis* – which indicates the act of 'discernment', of 'judgment' – and the Latin word *discrimen* – which means 'decision/division' – would be explained.[15] At the present stage of research, the origins of the term are uncertain. It remains revealing, however, that even the hypothesis of a derivation from the verb *keiro* – advanced by Van Windekens[16] – brings it back to the semantic family of the 'caesura'. Furthermore, this meaning would allow us to shed light on both the Platonic and the Aristotelian concepts of time.

For Plato, *chronos* is the true imitation of *aión* in the sense of a division, a *rhythmic* articulation of duration. It is like a reproduction by snapshots of the continuum of a movie plot. It is a *necessary* division, given that the two sides – as already mentioned – sustain each other. None of them can do without the other: as André Breton stated, eternity always looks for a watch . . . therefore, neither side can be 'rescued' by instantiating the other aside, the same way that it is impossible to extract the continuity of a movie plot from the single frames that make it up. Taken individually, these would have no meaning, which they gain from the cinematographic narration as a whole. At the same time, however, the comprehensive sense of plot would not be possible without the imperceptible division in frames. Going further with this metaphorical profanation of such a sublime text, we could even argue that the unitary duration of the *aión* ('persisting in the One') is to the rhythmic succession of *chronos* as the 'paradigmatic' stage of assembling is to the snapshots of the film sequence. Metaphor aside: for Plato, because the two moments *belong to each other*, the 'chronological' dimension is not only a legitimate and necessary articulation of the 'aionic' dimension; it is also *eternal*. This is a necessary consequence of the premise: if the *mímesis* enacted by *chronos*, which 'proceeds according to the number', is a necessary complement of the eternal duration of *aión*, then the 'imitation' must be as eternal as the Model (*paràdeigma*).

As a matter of fact, in the excerpt under examination here, the complete definition of *chronos* is of a 'mobile' and – at the same time – 'eternal' image of *aión*. In the Platonic definition of time, then, besides the noun *aión*, a decisive role is played by the adjective *aiónos*. Let us read, then, the whole sentence: 'And He [i.e., the *patér-poietés*, the Demiurge creator of the world according to the *paràdeigma*] then thought to create a mobile image of eternity and, at the same time as he called forth the Sky, he created an eternal image, that proceeds according to the number, of the permanent *aión* in the One: that which we call *chronos* [*eikò d'epenoei kinetón tina aionos poiesai, kai diakosmón ama ouranòn poièi ménontos aionos en enì kat'arithmòn iousan aionion eikona, touton on de chronon onomakàmen*]'.[17]

If we want to deal appropriately with the extraordinary power of these words, we must resist the temptation of reading them according to the numerous neo-Platonic dualisms – which are fundamentally simplified and reductive. In these, the 'black box' of the soul controls the flows of the *exitus* and *reditus*, through which the Great Drama of the exit into the multiple, and the return into the One, is performed. At the same time, however, it works as a bridge between the two 'levels' – that of time and that of a-temporal Eternity – that are, ultimately, separated and incommensurable.[18] Indeed, when commenting this passage from the *Timeus*, Plotinus omits the expression *kat'arithmòn iousa*.[19] It is a telling omission, given that it is precisely while proceeding according to number that Chronos constitutes itself as the eternal image – as well as the necessary ontological articulation – of Aión, which, instead, remains in the One.

Herein lies the profoundly innovative and ultimately revolutionary character of this Platonic conclusion: *chronos* is as eternal as *aión*. Both are either 'always' together or fall *together*.

3

Einstein's dream

We now turn to the reductionism implicit in the rebuttal of chronological time as proposed by the philosophies of 'authentic' temporality. It is not a coincidence that today's sophisticated cosmologies of the 'time's arrow' refer to Bergson's '*vécu*' in order to contest the 'classical' determinism of Einstein's relativity. As Ilya Prigonine and Isabelle Stengers polemically stated, in *Entre le temps et l'éternité*, 'a science that tries to reconstruct the objective truth of phenomena starting from an intelligible but a-temporal reality will certainly be unable to understand Bergson's "intimate experience of time".'[1]

In relation to this notion of authenticity, I will then confess to my attachment to the German word *Erfarhung* (greater than that to the abused term *Erlebnis*, which implies the 'presumed innocence' of inner awareness, as if the latter were capable of a direct grasp of 'existence'). In *The Arrow of Time* – containing an enthusiastic preface by Prigogine himself – Peter Coveney and

Roger Highfield seem to go even further, by reinstating common sense, that which Bergson himself used to call the 'ordinary perception' of time:

> We all note the irreversible flow of time, which seems to dominate our existence, in which the past is unchangeable and the future is open. We may wish to turn back the clock, to erase the mistakes we have made or to re-live a wonderful moment of our past. But, unfortunately, common sense tells us that this is not possible: time, like the tide, waits for no one. Time cannot go backwards. Or is the reverse true? It is unfortunate that this common notion of time has little credit in many scientific theories, where the direction of time is not considered very important. Newton's mechanics, Einstein's relativity and Heisenberg's and Schrödinger's quantum mechanics, which constitute the foundations of modern science, would work just as well if time went backwards. For these theories, the events recorded on a film would be plausible independently from the fact that it is showed forwards or backwards. The unidirectional character of time, then, seems to be a mental deception. With a slightly derisive tone, scientists dealing with this issue often define our daily perception of time as 'psychological' or 'subjective' time.[2]

The limit of Einstein's theory of time – which is similarly present in Bohr's, Heisenberg's and Schrödinger's quantum mechanics, despite their incompatibilities and differences – would seemingly consist in its detachment from daily experience. This detachment would lead the theoretical foundations of relativity, of the metaphysics of quanta, and of the indeterminacy principle, to a paradoxical *indifference* towards the direction of time; that is, to a lack of distinction 'between the time that flows forward and the time that flows backward'.[3] We find here a first problem, however: is such an emphatic rehabilitation of common sense a truly valid alternative to those conceptions? Does it not it run the risk of eliminating from them the element that made them revolutionary and path-breaking in the first place, that is, the paradox of the contemporary presence of symmetry and asymmetry within the four-dimensional continuum of time and space?

The term *paradox* should be understood in a 'strong' sense here: in its etymological sense of 'opposed to *doxa*', to *communis opinio*. Einstein used it in this very sense in the memorable pages of his *Scientific Autobiography* that follow his touching relinquishment of Newton's ideas:

> And now enough. Newton, forgive me; in your time, you found the only path possible for a man of the highest intellect and creative power. The concepts you established still guide our thoughts in the field of physics, even if we now know that they will have to be replaced with others, which are *much more distant from the realm of immediate experience*, if we

> want to reach a *deeper knowledge of the relations among things.*[4]

From a philosopher's point of view, the last words of this passage (which are here emphasized) are the most important in the whole sentence: in order 'to reach a deeper knowledge of the relations among things' it is necessary to replace Newton's concepts with 'other' concepts, which are much more distant, in common sense, from the 'realm of immediate experience'. During the past years a lot of discussion, whether appropriate or not, has gone on about the 'philosophical implications' of relativity theory.[5] Nevertheless, it seems that one fact has eschewed serious reflection: the *deeper* level mentioned in the above sentence does not imply any 'essentialist' formulation. To argue such a conclusion would in fact be a contradiction, given that Einstein himself recognized that the *philosophical* works of two great critics of essentialism – David Hume and Ernst Mach – guided him in the clarification of the paradox of special relativity. Suffice it to recall the engaging statement that closed Moritz Schlick's essay *Raum und Zeit in der gegenwärtigen Physik*, already back in 1917:

> We recognize the huge theoretical potential of the new conceptions: Einstein's analysis of the concepts of time and space belongs to the same line of philosophical development as David Hume's rebuttal of the representations of substance and causality. How this evolution will carry on, it is impossible

> to say. Its prevailing method, however, is the only fruitful one in the theory of knowledge: a rigorous criticism of the fundamental concepts of science, which eliminates all that is superfluous and brings to light their authentic and definitive content.[6]

The word 'deep', then, seems to allude to something else: to an 'oneiric', *unconscious* dimension that, according to Einstein, is always in an enigmatic relation with thought and the 'free play of concepts' from which, ultimately, the formalized language of science itself derives. A hint at this theme could already be found in a reference to the *Unbewusst*, to the 'unconscious', which is present in the same passage in which Einstein introduces the subject of the *paràdoxon*.[7] Many years before, during a conference held in Tokyo in 1922, he had stated: 'it is not easy for me to explain how I arrived at the relativity theory, because human thought is inspired by many complex and hidden factors, and because such factors act in different measure'.[8] Now, during the scientist's autobiographic assessment (and, one could say, self-critical, had the term not been largely corrupted) this same theme is reconsidered and further developed. Let us then see the whole sentence, which is very important in order to grasp both the embryo and the birth of the new conception.

At the beginning of this century – that is, shortly after 'Planck's prescient work' – Einstein had reached the conclusion that neither mechanics nor thermodynamics could claim absolute validity:

> Little by little, I started to despair of the possibility of finding true laws through attempts based on known facts. The longer and the more desperately I tried, the more I convinced myself that only the discovery of a *universal formal principle* could have led us to certain results. Before me was the example of thermodynamics. The general principle was all contained in this statement: the laws of nature are such, that it is impossible to build a *perpetuum mobile* [...]. But how could we find such a universal principle? After ten years of reflections, such a principle resulted from a *paradox* that I encountered when I was sixteen years old: if I could follow a ray of light having speed *c* (the speed of light in a vacuum), this ray of light would appear, in the state of rest, as an electromagnetic field oscillating in space. Yet, nothing similar seems possible based on Maxwell's experiments or equations. Since the start, it seemed to me intuitively clear that, from the point of view of such an imaginary observer, all should happen according to the same laws that are valid for an observer that is still in relation to the Earth. Otherwise, how could the first observer know, that is, how could he establish that he is in a state of very fast uniform motion?[9]

The speed of light – or of an electromagnetic wave – *in a vacuum* is, therefore, a *natural constant*: a *universal* physical constant that is independent from any parameter and whose value, then, is the same in any system of reference. This is equivalent to assuming the principle that, in nature, no signal – and, therefore, no body – can move faster than the speed of light (whose constant is a precise value: c = 300,000 km/sec). This paradoxical consequence of the relativity principle constitutes the determining element of the whole theory: 'It is clear', writes Einstein, 'that this paradox already contains the seeds of special relativity'.[10] But, in order to understand this paradox, another decisive step was necessary: 'patricide'. That is, it was necessary to demonstrate the arbitrary character of the Newtonian axiom of absolute Time, of the time that 'flows uniformly and that is otherwise called duration'; to undermine that postulate of simultaneity for which there exists an 'at present', a 'now' that all individuals experience at the same moment, independently from their position in space. As any patricide, this one also presumed the identification and unveiling of a heritage long rooted in unconsciousness:

> Naturally, everybody today knows that any attempt to clarify in a satisfactory way this paradox was doomed to fail, as long as the axiom of the absolute character of time, that is, of simultaneity, *remained unconsciously rooted, without us realizing it*. To recognize clearly this axiom and its arbitrary nature precisely means to solve this problem. Reading the philosophical writings of David Hume and Ernst Mach made

the type of critical reasoning necessary for the discovery of this core point much easier for me.[11]

We will come back later to the general meaning of this shift, thanks to which, while that which was absolute in the Newtonian universe becomes relative (space and time), that which was relative becomes absolute (so that the factor *c*, the universal constant of the speed of light, ends up gaining the a-temporal prerogatives of Plotinus' *lumen divinum*, but in the form of *lumen naturale*). For the time being, I would like to reflect on the role that the reference to the dimension of 'dreams' and 'wonder', as the original site of any creation and rational construction, played in Einstein. This point, which is as decisive as much as it is neglected, allows us to shed light on the link posed between the symbolic basis and the conventional character of scientific theories by Einstein's reflection.

'What is "thought", precisely?' asks Einstein. The answer is unequivocal: the origins of thought should not be placed in an autonomous 'ability', neither should they be attributed to an *actus purus*; to the contrary, they should be sought in the associative dynamics engendered by memory and imagination. Briefly put: *image* and *concept* form an inextricable network. Yet, the surfacing of certain images in memory, due to the input of sensorial impressions, is not yet 'thought'. Neither is it thought, when images evoke one another, thus forming a sequence. Thought only begins when an image is repeated in many sequences, becoming – through iteration – an 'ordering element' that 'links sequences that, in themselves, would not be connected'.[12] The ordering element thus becomes a tool, a *concept*. Therefore, between the original, or 'spontaneous' and, ultimately, 'oneiric' forms of association and properly conceptual constructions there is no break, but rather transition:

> I think that the passage from free association, or 'dream', to thought is characterized by the more or less dominating function that the 'concept' takes on in it. It is not at all necessary for a concept to be linked to a sign that is recognizable and reproducible through the senses (a word); however, when this happens, thought becomes communicable.[13]

All our thoughts, according to Einstein, are characterized by this 'free play of concepts'. And this play is justified by the greater or lesser support that it can give in the attainment of 'a general vision of sensorial experience'.[14] Starting from these premises, then, what happens to the notion of 'truth'? In this case too, Einstein's answer leaves no room for misunderstanding:

> The notion of 'truth' cannot yet be applied to this mechanism: in my view, this concept can only be taken into consideration when there already is a general agreement (a *convention*) on the elements and the rules of the game.[15]

Emphasis on the two extremes of associative dynamics of images and conventional character of scientific truth – connected through the 'clearing house' of iteration and the 'free play of concepts' – would seem to exclude any form of naïve objectivism and determinism. On the other hand, we know that Einstein's model is not at all devoid of 'causal thinking' – as confirmed by the scientist's dispute with Niels Bohr and the so-called 'Copenhagen interpretation' of quantum mechanics. We were all surprised by the account of Abraham Païs who was asked, while discussing quantum theory with Einstein: 'Do you really believe that the Moon exists only when we are looking at it?'.[16] Yet, in Einstein, a stress remains on the open, richly traumatic and 'perturbing' character of scientific discoveries – independently from the dubious results of his final attempt at reaching a unified theory of the 'field' (which deeply affected philosophers). This is another one of the 'secret threads' of his reflection, which can be identified particularly in the way he treats side by side the theme of 'unconsciousness' and that – exquisitely philosophical – of *thaumazein*, of 'wonder':

> For me, there is no doubt that our thought proceeds, for the most part, without the use of signs (words), and, very often, unconsciously. How can it otherwise be that we 'marvel' in such a spontaneous way at some experiences?[17]

But how – and when – does the *thauma* manifest itself? 'Wonder', replies Einstein, manifests itself through a clash, a fundamental conflict that is at the basis not only of any 'growth' but, above all, of any authentic quality leap in the knowledge of reality. It manifests itself through the conflict in which experience (*Erfahrung*) opposes 'a world of concepts that is already sufficiently stable in us'.[18] The theme of the paradox thus re-surfaces. This time, however, against the scientific *doxa* itself, intended as an institutionalized system of 'beliefs' that have consolidated through time and that have taken root in our sub-consciousness through habit. Indeed, every time we 'experience such a conflict in an acute and intense way, our intellectual world reacts with determination'.[19] We can then state – concludes Einstein – that the autonomous 'development of such an intellectual world', the self-sufficiency of its language and of its systems of certainties, 'is, in some sense, a continual escape from "wonder"'.[20]

It is difficult – for a non-specialist like me – to assess whether and to what extent the cosmological 'visions' of the time's arrow scholars represent a *thauma* in relation to a relativity that has, by now, become a fossilized and unsuitable model, or, rather, an instance of the 'escape from wonder'. The fact remains, however, that precisely the pioneering work carried out by Stephen Hawking and Roger Penrose, between 1965 and 1970, demonstrated that relativity theory is anything but dead. Einstein did not foresee the possibility of a dynamic cosmological model able to consider the *particularity* of the Big Bang and the Big Crunch – Genesis and Apocalypse. Yet, it is beyond doubt that one can arrive at those particularities (that is, the points of space-time whose 'volume' is, respectively, zero and infinite mass) precisely starting from the equations of general relativity. According to Hawking's point of view, the time of general relativity is only 'a coordinate that labels the events of the universe', which 'has no meaning outside the variety of space-time'. To question what was or what happened *before* the Big Bang, before the universe started, would be like 'looking for a 91 degree latitude point on Earth', a point that is simply undefined and indefinable. For this reason, instead of talking of 'the creation of the universe and of its possible end, one should say: "The universe exists".'[21] According to Penrose, the Oxford mathematician that first studied 'particularities', the fact that Einstein's conceptions do not consider the evolution of the universe from the Big Bang to the (possible) Big Crunch is not a good reason for discarding the concept of relativity. Those who think of using particularities to show that the theory of general relativity is simply wrong and irreversibly obsolete do not realize that 'the strength of relativity lies precisely in the fact that it is able to indicate its own limits'.[22] Penrose's argument is that the problems created in physics by the study of particularities are such, that they suggest a synthesis between relativity and quantum micro-physics as a possible solution. As we know, Einstein did not accept as definitive the abandonment of causality implicit in quantum mechanics. This abandonment, however, would now seem to offer a solution to the difficulties encountered by relativistic physics.

The latter is valid for very large distances – on a cosmological scale – where it replaces Newton's physics, while it must be replaced by quantum theory in the realm of elementary particles (atoms and molecules).[23] For very obvious technical reasons, this is not the right place for an analysis of the scientifically most shocking aspects of this 'neo-synthesis', which are represented by the theory of 'quantum gravity'. Therefore, I will limit myself to summarizing those aspects that – according to Penrose himself – are the richest in philosophical implications.

4

The cosmic dance of the mind

a. Universe and awareness

The first of these aspects relates to a very diffuse stereotype: that of the *strong* discontinuity between the classical model and quantum theory as regards the reality of the 'external' world. According to classical physics – from Newton to Maxwell and Einstein – the external world would have an objective reality and would evolve in a deterministic way, 'governed by very precise mathematical equations'.[1] This physical reality would exist objectively and independently from us, that is, from our *observation* criteria. The revolutionary innovation introduced by quantum microphysics, then – still according to that stereotype – would consist in the inversion of the realistic postulate of the classical model, which would make the external world a product, or a dependent variable, of *observation*. The subjective intervention of the observer, in other words, would modify the domain of the observed object to such an extent, that the very idea of 'objective reality' would be irreversibly compromised. While harshly contesting this stereotype, Penrose states that 'any "serious" philosophical point of view should, at the very least, contain a good degree of realism'. Clearly, this does not mean to reinstate *sic et simpliciter* the classical notion of reality, but rather to *re-define* it in such terms that both classical physics and quantum mechanics regain that degree of internal complexity that was inevitably sacrificed in their abstract juxtaposition.

The expression 'quantum theory' often recalls

> Simply the vague idea of an 'indeterminacy principle' that, at the level of particles, atoms or molecules, forbids the precision of our descriptions and simply establishes a probabilistic behaviour.

In reality, quantum descriptions are very precise, even if they are radically different from the familiar ones of classical physics; on the other hand, the latter are far less naïve than what the supporters of a strong discontinuity argument would have us believe. According to Penrose, the truly innovative – and richly destabilizing – power of quantum mechanics consists in that modification of our notion of physical reality, capable of encompassing even the phenomenon of the mind and of 'consciousness'. But, precisely for this reason, such an innovation, if adequately developed, must consider an *enlarged concept of reality*, capable of placing the mind within physical laws that *actually* govern 'the world we live in'. Taking up a famous a suggestion by Erwin Schrödinger[2] – who, however, is *not* quoted in this context – the Oxford mathematician states that the true limit of the classical universe, *despite its richness and mystery*, does not consist in a generic 'determinism' or 'causal reasoning' but, rather, in its inability to explain the phenomenon of conscience, which ends up representing either the *algorithm of the mind* – which evolves according to the same deterministic equations that govern 'objects' – or the unsolvable polarity of the *Subject* facing the World 'from the outside'. Here is Penrose's reasoning:

> The phenomenon of awareness could be incomprehensible in purely classical terms. Indeed, our mind could be a quality rooted in some strange and marvelous character of those physical laws that *actually* govern the world we live in, rather than being just a character of some algorithm translated into practice by the so-called 'objects' of a *classical* physical structure. Perhaps, in some sense, this is the 'reason' for which we, as conscious beings, must live in a quantum world, rather than in a wholly classical one, despite all the richness, and indeed the mystery, that are already present in the classical universe.

If 'a classical world is not something that awareness can be a part of', then consciousness can only depend on 'specific departures from classical physics'. It is for this simple but decisive 'reason' that the very existence of *observers*, of 'thinking and conscious beings such as ourselves' *calls for* a quantum world:

> We must indeed deal with quantum theory – the most exact and mysterious physical theory – if we want to analyze in depth *some of the most important philosophical issues*: how does our world behave, and what constitutes the 'minds', that is, in practice, 'ourselves'?

The acquisition of a 'deep philosophical idea' of the realities we live in calls for a comparison with 'existing quantum theory'. At the same time, according to Penrose, the argument that there is no reality but in relation to measurement and calculus procedures is 'too defeatist'; therefore, he attributes an *objective physical reality* – the *quantic state* – to quantistic descriptions. However, when determining the temporal evolution of the quantic state – which is expressed in rigorously deterministic terms through *Schrödinger's equation* – we do not only face the difficulties represented by 'quantum leaps', for which, each time that we perform a 'measurement' we must take into account (that is, *calculate*) that the given state leaps to one or another of the possible new states (thus operating on the basis of a *probabilistic* interpretation of that equation that Schrödinger never accepted).

We also face another and more fundamental problem: for 'a 'measurement' to actually take place, the presence of a conscious being is necessary', that is, the presence of human observers that are 'themselves arguably made of minute quantic components'.

The 'awareness' phenomenon is thus separated from its merely psychological dimension, and is taken as an active component of the paradoxes of quantic measurement and calculations.[3] The consequences of such an assumption are not only physical-cosmological; they are specifically philosophical. The mind is not an inexplicable 'psychic event', neither is it the 'fortuitous' by-product of a complicated calculation: it is not, in other words, the algorithm of Artificial Intelligence. It is, rather, the 'phenomenon thanks to which we know the very existence of the universe'. To state this means to accept certain consequences. First, it means to argue that awareness is the only phenomenon able 'to endow a presumed "theoretical" universe with real existence'; it also means to derive from this that 'a universe governed by laws that do not admit awareness is no universe at all'; finally, it means to conclude that the separation of 'subject' and 'object', 'internal' and 'external' reality, I and World, belongs to a dualist superstition that has long been present in the philosophical (and scientific) Western tradition. So far, these seem to be the most mature and recent conclusions of contemporary physical-mathematical research. But what are the consequences of these 'serious' conclusions on the notion of time?

b. Penrose's mill

In this regard – and I deal here with the second aspect that I wanted to analyze – Penrose appears to be much more careful than the 'time's arrow' theoreticians. The 'feel of time's flow' certainly has a key role in our 'feelings of awareness': we do have 'the *impression* that we are always moving forward, from a well-defined past to an uncertain future'. This is, however, an *impression*, not a 'deeper' and more 'authentic' dimension. We should then fight the temptation of making both our perception and our 'internal sense' of time ontological: 'Awareness is, after all, the only phenomenon, that we know of, according to which time needs to "flow"!'. The way in which time is treated and considered in modern physics 'is not essentially different from that in which *space* is treated'. The time of physical descriptions 'in reality, does not "flow" at all'. Yet, according to our perceptions or sensations, 'time *flows*'. How can this happen?

> I argue – replies Penrose – that here, as well, there is something of an illusion, and that the time of our perceptions 'in reality' does not flow forward in the linear way in which we perceive it (whatever this might mean!). The temporal order that we 'seem' to perceive is, according to me, something that we impose on our perceptions in order to give them some sense in relation to the forward uniform temporal advancement of an external physical reality.

It is impossible to grasp the meaning of this conclusion unless we take into account the role played by references to 'Plato's world' in Penrose's thought, that is, references to those 'mathematical ideas' that allow us to discover the *paradoxical* configuration of the universe. Mathematical truths are indeed not *inventions*, but *discoveries*: they are not 'arbitrary constructions of the human mind' but they incredibly seem to correspond to the profound structures of reality, just like Benoît B. Mandelbrot's *set* (the Polish-American mathematician that formulated Fractal Theory).[4] Hence the need to revalue Plato's classical model that – half a century before Euclid's *Elements* – had had the brilliant intuition of the 'pre-existence' of mathematical concepts and of the secret correspondence (truthfully, of a Pythagorean origin) between the Number and the universal functioning of the Cosmos:

> Thanks to some miraculous intuitive perception, Plato, based on indications that had to be very rare at the time, seems to have foreseen, on the one hand, that mathematics should be studied and understood in itself, without asking for it to be totally and exactly applicable to the objects of physical experience; on the other hand, that the functioning of the external real world can be ultimately understood only in terms of an exact mathematics: that is, in the terms of the Platonic world of ideas, which is 'accessible through the intellect'.

It is interesting to note the convergence between this striking revaluation of Plato, in the midst of post-relativistic physical enquiry, and the reinstatement of Plato's 'arithmosophia' as carried out, in a wholly different context, by Giorgio de Santillana and Hertha von Dechend – with their evocative research on the myth and structure of time, entitled *Hamlet's Mill.*[5] Ancient Greek philosophers and cosmologists, defined by the authors as 'our forefathers', certainly built their vision of the World starting from an idea that, for us, is outdated and false: the geocentric universe. They reached 'speculative conclusions on the destiny of the soul within a cosmos where present geography and science of the heavens are still intertwined today'. They derived – which is an even more serious fact – the laws of Kosmos from the 'apparent movement of stars', from 'pure kinematics'. Finally, they founded their theoretical construction on 'a conception of time very different from the modern one, which is metric, linear and monotone'. Yet – despite these limitations – their perspective appears, today, surprisingly fruitful:

> Those forefathers of ours had not only made time a structure, a cyclical time; they had also developed the creative idea that the Number was the secret of all things. In saying that 'things are numbers' they embraced in a huge arch the whole set of astronomic and mathematical ideas from which, one day, real science would have originated. It is those unknown geniuses

who set the guidelines for modern thought, that perceived its evolution; but their ideas were at least as complex as ours today. Cosmological Time, the 'dance of stars', as Plato called it, was not a simple angular measure, an empty repository, as it is today, of the so-called history (those scary and meaningless surprises that people have resigned themselves to call *fait accompli*). It was believed that it was powerful enough to exert an inflexible control over events, shaping them according to its own sequences in a cosmic system where past and future called one another, from depth to depth. Grand and fearful, the Measure repeated and echoed the structure in many ways, it marked Time, it was the source of inexorable decisions that determined the 'expiration' of a given moment.[6]

There are indeed many more things between sky and earth than those included in the scheme 'from *mythos* to *logos*' or 'from the world of approximation to the universe of precision'...

From Einstein's 'dream' – helped by Santillana's myth and Penrose's mathematical world – we have come back to Plato's 'dream'. In conclusion, we may perhaps have more than one doubt about Penrose's argument, according to which mathematical *discoveries* are just a form of memory, in the Platonic sense of the *anàmnesis*, recollection of something *already-for-ever present* in the mind. We may perhaps ask serious questions over his attempt – that is, in fact, still underway – at reaching a neo-synthesis between general relativity and quantum theory. His idea of mathematical language as the key to penetrate the *paradoxes* of our universe, however – which is both Platonic and Einsteinian[7] – remains central. Similarly, his criticism of the notion of *temporal flow* is simply unavoidable.

And, in any case, it will be difficult to oppose, to these reasons, the 'revolutionary discovery' of the theoreticians of the arrow: 'time, like the tide, waits for no one'.

5

The architecture of time

The image of the 'flow', then, does not seem to render the fundamental nature of the temporal dimension and of the role that is played in it by the phenomenon of awareness. Yet, if it is true that, nowadays, science is the one to take charge of those *paradoxes* of temporality that neither Bergson's *durée* nor Husserl's *Erlebnisstrom*[1] – 'the flow of consciousness' – seem able to consider, what room should be given to philosophy? More generally: can philosophical reflection still play a role, besides the activity (that, ultimately, is purely residual) of linguistic, merely logical purification that it was assigned by Neo-positivism and by the various versions of analytical tradition? After a long and painful investigation into the 'question of time', I believe I have reached a fairly serious conclusion: the mode of thinking that – starting with Socrates – we have called 'philosophy' has no room left other than that of the, so to speak, 'archeological' deconstruction-reconstruction of some keywords of our lexicon, of the language with which, *in the West*, we have tried to order and govern our *particular* experience of the world for about 2,500 years. It is, however, a *very different role* from the function of meta-language of sciences that it was attributed by logical empiricism, or of 'foundational' clarification of the meaning of statements that it was given by analytical philosophy of language. By now, sciences are able to find their own 'foundation', by autonomously constructing their own grammars and logics (and, for this reason, they do not even need epistemologists, other than as 'sports announcers' of their own actual practices). The role of philosophy, then, should be sought elsewhere. Not in the field of foundation, but in that of *enquiry*: one that – as we will see shortly – addresses those difficulties, those uncertain junctions of our experience, which make up the inescapable premise and the common basis of any knowledge. The intersection of science and philosophy, then, is not at all between a philosophical science and a scientific philosophy (maybe made compatible by the epistemological 'clearing house'). It *can be*, rather, between a science that, *as science*, is able to produce philosophical implications, and a philosophy that, *as philosophy*, proves able to stimulate scientific enquiry – starting from *its own* questions. Still, the questions posed by philosophy, because they relate to *experience*, rather than *experiments*, cannot – let me repeat – but deal with the symbols, the metaphors, the keywords, the *boundary terms* with which we try to master the 'reality we live in'.

It is not a coincidence that the most recent results of interdisciplinary investigations into time have agreed on the strong influence of language on all the cultures of the planet: the influence exerted by the (ultimately etymological) variety of names with which the phenomenon of temporality is usually defined. It is such a macroscopic phenomenon that we often miss it, precisely because it is so near to us: we will, however, analyze it more deeply in the last part, when we will deal with the 'mystery' of the origins of the Latin word *tempus*. Another important aspect emerging from this study relates to the replacement of the metaphors of the 'stream' and the 'flow' with the notions of *architecture of time* and *topology of time*.[2] These notions are grounded on the realization that a concept of time modeled on our intuitive perception is insufficient:

> An understanding of time entirely based on intuition – argues Fraser – is totally inadequate for the complex structure of time as revealed by contemporary scientific thought. There is nothing intuitive in the statement that there is a hierarchy of temporality, that is, that there exist qualitatively different forms of time that are characteristic, respectively, of the world of light, of atomic particles, of matter endowed with mass

(that is, the world of stars and galaxies), of living organisms, of men's minds and of cultural systems. Yet, it is precisely a universal understanding of time that we should tend to because, as human beings, we belong to all the organizational levels of nature.[3]

In the topological-hierarchical articulation of the architecture of time, *five distinct temporalities* are commonly identified. These can be explained – starting from our level of experience – with the help of the arrow metaphor:

(1) *Noo-temporality*, or noetic time; it can be represented as a well-defined arrow, which includes an arrowhead, a shaft and a flight (that is, an arrow with direction). This image represents the kind of time that *exclusively* belongs to a mature human mind, to 'awareness': a time characterized by a clear and conscious distinction between past and future; by unlimited horizons of memory and expectation; and by a 'mental present' whose temporal boundaries are changeable according to the levels of attention.

(2) *Bio-temporality*, or biological time; it can be represented as an arrow whose arrowhead and flight are no longer well-defined, even if they are still distinct. This is the temporal reality of all living organisms (including men, as far as their biological functions are concerned). Here,

as well, there is a distinction between the three levels of time [past, present and future, *translator's note*], but in different measure according to the various living species; the 'mental' present of the noo-temporal level is replaced here with the 'organic present' of the life process.

(3) *Eo-temporality*, or the *t* of physicists; it can be represented as an arrow with neither arrowhead nor flight, thus reduced to a simple shaft, or straight line. It is the temporal reality of the astronomic universe of matter with a mass, or macroscopic physical universe. It is the most simple, in some sense initial, form of continuous time (its name, in fact, derives from Eos, the goddess of dawn). It is a time with no preferential direction (thus *bidirectional*) and no 'present' (hence also devoid of past and future).

(4) *Proto-temporality*, or the time of the subatomic universe of elementary particles; it can be represented as an arrow broken into disconnected parts. It is a time with neither direction nor continuity, for which the identification of precise moments is meaningless and it is also, in principle, impossible to distinguish a 'now', a 'before' and an 'after'. In the proto-temporal world, events can be located only in a statistical, probabilistic way.

(5) *A-temporality*, or the world of light and electromagnetic radiation; it can be represented as an arrow whose parts

> are fading. It is the time, literally reduced to zero, of the particles that move at the speed of light. The *a-temporal realm of light* represents the impassable frontier of time and, at the same time, the horizon of its complex architecture.

The contemporary enquiry on the physical world has not, therefore, led to the discovery of a Super-time, of an absolute Present but, rather, to the disintegration of the idea of a universal flow of time:

> There is nothing, in the physical world, to which this image of a moving present or of a time that flows can correspond. There is no ultimate speed at which the time of the universe flows, with which we can compare some inner sense of becoming. The origins of the sense of the passing of time, and of its abstract representation, must be exclusively sought in our mind.[4]

How does one place the dimension of *our* life, within such an 'estranging' picture, so shocking for the familiar certainties of common sense? What cosmic *clinamen* has favored the genesis of living forms and the birth of *our* time? Finally: what secret 'need' generates in us the impression of *one* direction of time?

In order to give some meaning – certainly not a solution – to these questions, we need to take a journey through the labyrinth of the Western notions of time, taking the same corridor, the same narrow passage from which philosophy had originally sprung: the corridor of experience and of the boundary terms with which classical physics-metaphysics, starting with Aristotle, had *desperately* tried to neutralize its paradoxes.

6

Philosophy: Eros' interlude

As we mentioned, the term 'experience' should be understood here in its sense of *Er-fahrung*, experience-journey, not in the sense of *Er-leben*, or *Er-lebnis*, experience-life.[1] Experience is an *er-fahren*: it is like *taking a journey*. For the same reason, it is necessary to refer also to the Greek term *em-peiría*, whose Latin equivalent, *ex-perientia,* is a faithful mould. *Em-peiría* indicates the movement through the narrow passages of the test, of the trial. And – a fact that is seldom considered – it derives from the same root as *per-iculum*.[2] These indications already show how little intimidated I am by some trendy, pseudo-intellectual notions, and how much I believe that philosophy should go back to its place of origin.

But here comes a question: what is this place? I will answer in a wilfully drastic way: it is, when looking closely, the same as the

Unheimlich, as that 'disorientating' or familiar stranger that is the core of Freud's work (that today, for the most part of contemporary psychoanalytic enquiry – and, I am afraid, also practice – seems reduced to little more than a ritual reference).[3] It is the site of the *metaxý*, introduced by Diotimus' oration, which is reported by Socrates in Plato's *Symposium*: '[It is] something in between wisdom and ignorance (*ti metaxý sophias kai amathias*)', between mortal and immortal (*metaxý thnetoú kai athanatou*), between human not-knowing and divine *sophía*.[4] The *dýnamis*, the capacity assigned to philosophy, therefore, shares the same nature and power as the 'demon', it is located in the same 'demoniac' place as Eros, the *daimon megas*. And, adds Diotimus, *to daimonion metaxý esti theoú te kai thnetoú*, 'the demoniac is in between the divine and the mortal'.[5] It is the site of the *interlude*, then. But, because of this, it is also the site of tension, of constitutive *dissatisfaction*: 'no god loves wisdom [literally: 'philosophizes', *philosopheí*] neither does he wish to become wise, for he already is; and, on the other hand, no wise man (*sophós*) philosophizes (*philosopheí*)'.[6] For this reason, *philosophía* is eternally struck by Eros' arrow: it can only be the love of something that one does not have. Its proper *dýnamis*, its virtue-power, is therefore the same as that of the demon: the *hermeneutic* function, the role of an interpreter-messenger that continuously produces the passage from one to the other dimension in which it precariously participates.[7] From this derives a first, decisive warning to philosophers: never pursue the fatal illusion of universal satisfaction, of the end of the exile as the definitive escape from the tension of the *metaxý*. Never turn the *daimon* into an *er-daimon*, thus turning the *daimonía* into the happy state of the *eu-daimonía*: because, once the exile is over, the *dýnamis*, the very power and *raison d'être* of the *philo-sophèin*, will also inevitably disappear. At the precise moment in which it claims to abolish tension and becomes a settlement on abstract models of Truth (as today happens to many, too many, intellectual notions), philosophy inevitably loses the 'eros' that should feed it – and that places it precisely in the lack of stability, in this *in-stant* between ignorance and knowledge. Hence, there is no philosophy other than as a desire of something that one can never own, similarly to a loved object. And the *philósophos*, more than anybody else, should know that a loved object, once owned, is no longer loved. He/she *should know* . . .

My reflection starts from the West, for the simple reason that the 'eros' rooted in the *philo-sophèin* is a product wholly particular to the West. There is no oriental philosophy in the proper sense, other than as a projection, on the East, of our 'identity' obsession. An obsession that is culturally determined, historically relative. But I will not go any further into this. Karl Jaspers explained in a definitive way how the very antithesis East-West is a cliché, a *topos* characteristic of Western civilization:

> Since the beginning, since the times of the Greek, the European world has been constituted by an *inner polarity* between the West and the East. Since Erodotus, there has been the awareness of an antithesis between East and West as of an eternal antithesis, which always appears in new forms. Only in so doing has this antithesis become real, because something becomes spiritually real only when it is known, not before. The Greek founded the world of the West, but in such a way that it keeps on existing only as long as it keeps its gaze on the East, compares itself with it, understands it and detaches itself from it, adopts its elements and re-elaborates them, up to the point of making them its own [. . .]. *This antithesis has always been a constitutive element of Europe, while the East has simply adopted it from the latter, and has understood it in the European sense.*[8]

The antithesis East-West is, therefore, an 'internal polarity' of the West; an original one, constitutive of Western identity. And because the 'East' is always a projection *of the West*, I am obliged to start my discussion from the latter.

I will, then, start from the West, but deal with a problem that transcends it: the assessment (or, better, the self-assessment) of its development, which entirely coincides with the development of philosophy. When I say 'transcend', I do not mean it in the sense of a 'post-philosophical' attitude *à la* Richard Rorty (who – with a position that is wholly indefensible today – declares himself 'an associate of the poet rather than of the physicist'[9]), nor in the sense of the *Überwindung/Verwindung*, that is, of the 'going beyond Nihilism' as argued by Gianni Vattimo, whose *rhetoric of the beyond* I disagree with (this is not a polemic note since – as is well known – 'weak thought' uses the word *rhetoric* with a positive connotation[10]). Rather, it should be understood as a *philosophie éclatée*,[11] which implies the need to radically 'put into question' the 'Logos' of the identity grounding Western philosophical tradition. This should not necessarily be done in the 'manneristic' way in which the question of logo-centrism, in fact, of logo-phono-centrism, was dealt with by Derrida (and by those who, more or less knowingly, follow his path).

The philosophy that 'sprang', that came out of its apodictic-sapiential shell has, by now, become aware of the intrinsically subversive character of its very place of origin, of that original 'friction' (as Wittgenstein would have called it) that any logo-centrism removes as a condition of its own constitution. But this place – it should be noted – can no longer be that of the 'paradox', now the constitutive premise of any serious scientific enquiry and theory. It is, rather, the place of *aporia*. A-poria indicates the not-being-able-to-pass, the being-without-escape. A proper philosophy can only be, today, one that avoids 'solutions', engaged in the search for blocked paths. However, the method of the *aporia*, if radically followed, will only produce a deflagrated philosophy. To move from such an option – I realize – means to go against the enlightening 'highway' philosophies that populate the postmodern cultural scene: I am thinking, in particular, of the all-knowing aspiration of those current 'sports announcers' of science that we call epistemologists. I am convinced that their 'constructs' represent an obstacle more than a means of comparison between philosophical reflection and a science that effectively works and does research. Of these sciences, psychoanalysis is undoubtedly an essential component, not despite, but precisely by virtue of its periodic 'constitutional crises'. In stating this, I must necessarily take two things for granted (while they still constitute a matter of debate between the various psychoanalytical 'schools' and 'currents of thought'): 1) there is no 'psychoanalytic theorem' in the sense of a coherent system of statements or unitary theoretical-practical set;[12] there is, rather, a constellation of gravitational centers (starting from the notions of *Unheimlich* and *Unbewusst*, the 'disorientating' and the 'unconscious'), which have already contributed to undermine the notions of Subject and Object, Identity and Presence, and that clearly may be further developed and deepened; 2) psychoanalytic work, while operating with its own tools (which are those of the medical practice and of therapeutic techniques) occupies the same place as the *philo-sophèin*, the zone-limit, or the interlude, of the *metaxý*. The best definition of this amphibious nature of psychoanalysis, I think, is given by Ernst Gellner in his *Tractatus Sociologicus-Philosophicus*:

> Psychoanalysis owes its charm to the fact of being at once a part of science, through medicine, while affirming – in fact, reinforcing – the importance of what is intimately personal and immediate, the value and meaning of *participation*. Its theories-interpretations all belong both to the technical mystery of science, and to the noisy immediacy of everybody's most personal experience. Briefly put, the ideological vigor and the intense charm of those doctrines that are situated on this particular boundary line eloquently attest to the importance of that great juxtaposition in our intellectual life.[13]

We will deal more in detail with this 'boundary population' later. For the moment, we should go back to that labyrinth passage that had led us to the experience of the *philo-sophèin*.

The path of philosophizing, as an *er-fahren*, is constituted as a learning process. I would add: *a learning process with deadly results for the identity fetish*, including for the identity of philosophy. The crucial passage of this journey, then, should be named with courage and without any useless introduction: the failure of the ontological perspective in relation to the *Zeitfrage*, the question of time. To adopt such a definition – which is also a ruthless diagnosis of Western knowledge – means to fully attack, thus depriving them of their foundation, some serious (i.e., 'heavy') statements on the ontological priority of time over space, which are present not only in the philosophers of *authentic time*, such as Bergson, Husserl and Heidegger but also – which is even harder to understand – in scientists such as Ilya Prigogine or René Thom himself (who, on more than one occasion, has nonchalantly argued that time should be attributed a 'higher ontological depth than space'). Moving from this background, I will now briefly run through the *leit motif* of my recent reflection.

7

Familiar strangeness

a. To utter and to suffer

Time places itself at the crux of the relation between daily experience and its representation. From time immemorial, one of the main themes of Western metaphysics and philosophical speculation, the dimension of time permeates each moment of our lives. Yet, it is very difficult to produce communicable knowledge about it. Herein lie the origins of the *temporal paradox*, the intertwinement of *natural* and *enigmatic*, *obvious* and *inexplicable*, which characterize it. Time is, indeed, a *familiar stranger*.

The temporal paradox was identified with incredible clarity by Saint Augustine, in the famous sentence of the 14th chapter of Book XI of his *Confessions*: 'Quid est ergo tempus? Si nemo ex me quaerat, scio; si quaerenti explicare velim, nescio (What is, then, time? If nobody asks me, I know; if I must explain it to those who question me, I do not know)'.[1] In the identification of this paradox, the linguistic aspect of the problem must also be taken into account – as aptly understood by Paul Valéry; this is represented by the *false obviousness* of what we mean, every time we use the word *time*:

> What is Time? – It is a *word*; which explains why Saint Augustine knew what it is when he was not thinking about it, and stopped knowing when he did. He thought of this word, through this word, that is, he tried to replace an expedient with a *clear idea*.[2]

Our discourses on time, then, seem inexorably constrained by the words we use to convey a *pathos*, an 'attachment': an ineffable *feel* of time.

According to a theme that is dominant in the XX century philosophy of time (suffice it to refer to the already mentioned examples of Bergson, Husserl and Heidegger), our experience of time would be bound by the juxtaposition between an *authentic*, yet ineffable, time, which expresses the subjective and inner feel of duration; and an *inauthentic*, but measurable, time, which manifests itself in its objective and spatialized representation. In the first case, we would be dealing with the qualitative and incommensurable dimension of vitality; in the second, with the quantitative and measurable dimension of exteriority, which is homogeneous and indifferent to contents.

On the other hand, a specific pathogenesis of temporality is inherent in modern experience (I have already examined it in a previous work).[3] This pathogenesis derives from the split between, on the one hand, the wealth of possibilities opened by the technical-scientific project of control of nature (and of rationalization of social evolutionary processes) and, on the other, the poverty of its experience. A phenomenon of *acceleration* is thus produced (which, genealogically, can be traced back to the Hebraic-Christian roots of Modernity); due to this, time splits between an endless projection towards the future and the atrophy and fossilization of the past, which progressively erodes the space of existence of the present. The temporal split that is opened between experience and expectation, between the finite nature of time and the infinity of desire, also describes the impossible correspondence between the individual life and the temporal flow of the world.[4] On the one hand, indeed, the temporal flow of the world precedes and outlives individual life, thus showing the inevitability of the splitbetween existence and project. On the other hand, 'asynchronies' inevitably arise within Historical Time, times and rhythms that change according to the fields and domains of action. Two distinct problems of the 'modern condition' come to affect this phenomenon. The first relates to the theme of the 'crisis of the future'.[5] viewed as a consequence of the side-effects of the modern Project aimed at the planning of historical time and the 'colonization of the future'

(Octavio Paz): limits that are manifested in the latter's incapacity to understand the multiple and asynchronous, 'multi-versal' and stratified character or the architecture of time. The second relates to the pathology of acceleration, that Kant 'anthropologist' viewed as a characteristic of modern and, more generally, 'civilized men':

> To feel life, to amuse oneself, then, is nothing but to feel continuously pushed to *escape the present condition* (which, in turn, must be a pain that often returns). In this way, the oppressing and grievous ache given by boredom to all those who pay attention to their lives and time (civilized men) is also explained. This *drive to escape any moment of the time we are in*, and to pass onto the next, grows, and it can increase up to the decision to put an end to life itself [...]. The vacuum of sensations, felt in itself, engenders fear (*horror vacui*) and almost the presentment of a long death, which is considered more painful than fate giving a clean cut to the thread of life. This also explains why that which shortens time is considered one thing with pleasure: indeed, the more rapidly we pass time, and the more uplifted we feel.[6]

The need from which this thread of my reflection had originated, then, consisted in a search for new horizons of meaning for the experience of time, which would allow it to shield the opening towards the future from the sense of oppression with which it is experienced today. In this respect, discussions concerning 'the Beyond', as proposed by the various references to Nihilism, were not useful. In order to put the symbolic framework described in the previous pages into question, it was necessary to start from what had been *removed* by the post-modern 'overtaking', and further hidden in some sort of hyper-nihilistic shell, while wondering – thus 'reinstating' the spatial dimension – whether psychological time includes a mixture of both *symmetry* and *asymmetry* at the same time: a realm of co-presence, typical of space, and a realm of sequence, typical of chronological time. My reflection, then, stumbled upon the need for a prospective change of view; in fact, for a drastic *lateral shift*: from the problem of time going nihilistically adrift (typical of 'weak thought' and of post-modern philosophy in general) – or from the problem of the side-effects of the 'temporalization' of life domains (which was still at the center of my research on 'secularization') – to the problem of the (inextricably *spatial-temporal*) paradoxes of experience.[7]

What was the necessary procedure for this 'change of view', which recalls – and somehow presupposes – the Platonic 'shifting of gaze'? More generally: what philosophical reasons pushed me *to move the center of my enquiry from time to space*? These questions give me the opportunity to clarify some misunderstandings implied in some objections that arose, such as: the *pars destruens* of this statement is clear, less so the *pars construens*; does not such a proposal risk to lead to a metaphysical and/or science-like rehabilitation of spatiality? I will now address these objections, in reverse order.

b.1. 'Divine loquacity'

Countering the second type of objection is fairly easy: indeed, an author who dedicated an entire volume to the phenomenon of the 'temporalization' of historical *prágmata* – which is entirely Western and typically 'modern' – can hardly be accused of downplaying the dimension of time. The question that is worth dealing with, today, relates to the soundness of the so-called *secularization theorem*, understood as the simplified description of the presumed discontinuity between the 'cyclical time' of the classic and the 'linear time' of the modern, as well as the mechanic derivation of the notion of Progress from the Christian idea of Providence. Many important scholars, both Italian and foreign, have harshly criticized the secularization argument for being schematic: either because it would 'delegitimize' Modernity, by nullifying the historical, ethical-political and symbolic value of the 'Copernican revolution' (H. Blumenberg,[8] J. Habermas[9]); or because it would ignore the constant intertwinement of 'line' and 'circle', 'arrow' and 'cycle' that is present in both the classical and the modern visions of time (S. Mazzarino,[10] Paolo Rossi[11]). Yet, even these criticisms – which are certainly among the best documented and formulated – are prone to counter-criticism. For a start, how can we explain that that set of phenomena that go by the name of 'secularization' have *only* taken place in the Hebrew-Christian-origin West – as Max Weber had pointed out in his comparative studies?[12] How can we explain that – despite and independently from the polymorphic character of the representations of time – only the modern West has witnessed an *actual* socio-economic and technical-scientific development during the past two centuries, as well as the dominance of a way of planning that undoubtedly looks to the future? Was it a poor ideological scheme, or rather a detailed investigation into the origins of our culture that pushed a great scholar such as Leo Spitzer to locate the blueprint of all this in the "demusicalization' and secularization process that took place during the sixteenth and seventeenth centuries'?[13] Was it only an optical illusion leading Alexis de Tocqueville to state, at the end of his *Démocratie en Amérique*: 'I go through the centuries back to the furthest ancient times: I see nothing that looks like what stands before my eyes. Because the past no longer sheds light on the future, the spirit moves in the dark?'[14] Finally: do we really believe that the concept of secularization can be reduced to the thin and almost caricature-like 'theorem' to which it has been relegated by some of its critics, as much as by its supporters? Judging from the complexity of this debate, as well as from its most recent developments, the answer would seem to be negative. In fact, it is telling that, by now, the most radical versions of the 'secularization' idea tend *to stress precisely those themes that have traditionally represented the strong points of its harshest critics*: desacralization of the world and scientific *curiositas*; crisis of authority and individual autonomy; freedom of will and contingency.[15]

Christopher Lasch has recently gone to battle against the 'secularization argument'. Partly relying on Blumenberg, the American historian of ideas has criticized the secularization argument for 'hiding for too long the differences between the idea of Providence and the modern one of progress'.[16] This argument would reveal its weakness precisely where it is defended with the greatest force as in, for example, the work of Robert Nisbet.[17] In his attempt at pinpointing the roots of the idea of progress in Augustine and in the Fathers of the Church (besides classical authors such as Seneca and Lucretius), Nisbet would not realize that that idea is 'linked to a positive assessment of the proliferation of needs'[18]. But – as a curious but far from unusual *contrappasso* – the limit of the criticized position ends up being refracted in the eyes of the critic, thus impairing his view: what Lasch does not grasp, in his criticism, is that the secularization argument does not at all ignore the 'profound differences between the Christianprophetic and millenarian – vision of history and the modern conception of progress'.[19] The core of that argument – but in some of its providentialistic theological-historical versions – does not lie in the stubborn affirmation of continuity, but 'simply' in the indication that Judaism and Christianity encourage an *interest in history* that is absent in classical thought and in other cultures. Yet, acknowledging this and drawing from it the logical consequences would entail an operation that Lasch cannot, and, indeed, does not, perform: to place the *question of time* (and of the difference, which is truly radical, between a time that regenerates and a time that redeems) at the centre of attention. We can reason similarly concerning the other criticism, according to which the idea of progress, 'at least is its Anglo-American version', would have never centred around the notion of utopia, intended as the 'promise of an ideal society', 'heaven on earth', *true and only Heaven.*[20] As I think I have showed in my book on secularization,[21] starting from the end of the eighteenth century, utopia no longer plays a central role, and is replaced by *uchronia*, that is, the expectation of an indefinite and unlimited improvement. Are we really arguing that such a perspective is less projected into the future than the utopian one? If we do, we should base ourselves on arguments and documents that are much more convincing than those that Lasch used.

The criticism launched against the secularization argument by Ernst Gellner is more subtle and philosophically clever. It is more subtle because it dissociates the secularization paradigm from the traditionalist visions of history, linking its fate *exclusively* to the belief in 'divine loquacity', a belief that can be reconciled perfectly with the secular idea of an indefinite 'historical improvement':

> The singular thing is that, while secularization, the loss of faith and the scientific revolution eroded religion in Western societies, there was no need to relinquish, at the same time, the belief in the *loquacity of revelation*, in the demonstration of an ultimate truth through growth and repetition.[22]

Stated otherwise, the change in the specific *content* of history did not impose a relinquishing of the 'repetitive and loquacious *form*'; in fact, it emphasized it. The true wager of the secularization theorem, then, consists in taking, as its confirmation, precisely those events of modernity that its hasty critics considered the evidence of its blatant failure: first, 'the crystallization of faith in *progress*, in a continuing tale of historical improvement that gave meaning to men's efforts and counterbalanced human misery, thus representing a new and effective secular theodicy'; second, 'the formulation and acceptance of the idea of biological evolution, which more or less argued the same, even if in a greater (in fact, incomparably greater) representation.'[23] Assimilated by secularization, then, the notions of historical progress and biological evolution have turned into 'new sources of grandiose loquacious repetition, confirmation of a vision and its values.'[24] According to Gellner, therefore, in order to disprove the concept of secularization, it is not sufficient to focus on the presumed path-breaking value of this or that *content*, this or that historical-actual manifestation. It is necessary to undermine the *form* that sustains it, that is, the assumption of divine loquacity, the model of *revelation through repetition*. It is a difficult task, given that the same assumption is common to philosophies that are apparently rigorously 'secular' (such as those of Quine and Popper), and that support the argument of the *continuity* with, and the *derivation* from, some form of beginning, some matrix or embryo of Process.[25] The destruction of the idea of 'divine loquacity' – and of the 'Hegelianism' that is inherent to it, even if in an unconscious way – would entail, then, the definitive abandonment of the 'reiteration principle', even in its most radically secularized versions, which have 'critical method' and 'scientific spirit' derive from a coherent and unitary plot. Hence, it is necessary to state that 'God is not loquacious'; that 'history does not cumulatively repeat the same message'; that what differentiates the 'modern cognitive style' is not simply 'yet another performance of a repetition'.[26] As we can see, these are, once again, negations. What is, then, the point of view proposed by Gellner as an alternative to the repetition-revelation-secularization 'cartel'? It is the idea of the irreducible discontinuity and diversity of human visions, which is expressed through the concept of *cosmic exile*: 'The philosophy of cosmic exile has expressed well this discontinuity. The cosmic extra-territoriality of knowledge can only be a myth, while its historical discontinuity is not'.[27] Gellner's criticism of the secularization argument is certainly one of the most fascinating and focused that I have encountered.

But are we truly convinced that the ideas of discontinuity, pluralism and cosmic exile are able to overcome it? We have the impression that even this noteworthy case ignores the most radical versions of the 'theorem', in which all these themes are taken into account, and in which faith itself works as a paradoxical polarity, as an element of anxiety and heretical pluralization of the points of view. Ultimately, Gellner does not realize that, in order to keep the passage towards the 'paradox' clear, the postulates of 'divine loquacity' and of its 'revelation' through a smooth and coherent process are not at all necessary. A rigorous articulation of the secularization argument may also embrace the notions of discontinuity and cosmic exile, relinquishing the idea of a Becoming intended as a *pyramidal cumulativeness* that projects itself through time, providing definite parameters of choice of a valid 'vision', even in the ultra-secularized idea of scientific 'growth'.[28] The debate on this controversial category should proceed from here – against the backdrop of the cosmic disorientation and ethical contingency that mark the end of this millennium.

b.2. 'Negative theology of time'

We should now consider the objection of the 'first kind', relating to the relationship between the *pars destruens* and *pars construens* of the 'lateral shift' I proposed for a new interpretation of the question of time. I will start from the Talmudic quotation (in *hagigah* 2:1 of the *Mishnah*) I used in my previous book: 'Better would it be for he who thinks of these four things to never have been born – what lies above; what lies below; what is before; what is after.' Stated otherwise, for 'mortal issues' such as those of time and space, there are no *solutions*, but only *aporias*, blocked paths. Constructive procedures are not viable, and only *negative* ones are possible; in some sense, these are similar to the *rational negative theology* used by Maimonides to deal with the dilemma between the doctrine of creation and that of the eternity of the world in his *Guide for the Perplexed* (one of the key texts of Western thought).

Hence, *negative* theology of time.[29] But – one should note – *rational* negative theology. Maimonides believed he could not *demonstrate with a positive procedure* the act of creation but could only *rationally undermine* the arguments in favour of the idea of the eternity of the world.[30] Similarly, I do not pretend to 'solve' the eternal mystery of time; I will simply indicate its *aporia*, revealing the impossibility to conceive it outside references to spatial representations. Through a synthetic journey in the *labyrinths* of the classical and modern conceptions of time, therefore, I try to demonstrate how those philosophies that believe they have singled out the dimension of time in its purity are then forced to speak about it through references to images. Here, we are not only dealing with the differentiated origins of the ends that any program (whether scientific or philosophical) faces, every time that its operative application reveals the impractical nature of its axioms. We are dealing with a much more delicate and important phenomenon: a kind of *contrappasso,* for which time becomes pure externality whenever we try to grasp it in the authenticity of inner duration.

As we know, in § 258 of the *Enzyklopädie,* Hegel states that time does not reach the concept, because it is the abstract element of the *I* = *I* of pure self-awareness.[31] He also adds: not of pure self-awareness as such, but of pure self-awareness as limited to externality. The paradox identified by Hegel does not consist in saying that time is pure externality – that, in order to be relevant in philosophy, it must turn into a concept, hence deny itself as time, as the abstract form of the movement of awareness or, generally, of spirit. The paradox lies in stating that self-awareness becomes purely external the moment in which it declares its authenticity as a pure inner sense. Here is the core of the *contrappasso*: *precisely when we take refuge in a purely inner dimension, we inevitably encounter pure externality.* I believe that this phenomenon relates to the problem of the 'clash' between internal and external, which the most troubled and sensible part of post-Freudian psychology has struggled with.[32] The notion of 'clash' forces us to think of a profoundly important fact: psychoanalytic 'space' cannot be *sic et simpliciter* the locus of interiority; it must be the internal/external of unconsciousness, i.e., of something that, in relation to 'inner awareness', *produces a change of view*.

I believe that a similar need is present in the proposal of a *lateral shift* that I mentioned above. When I say *lateral* shift, I mean that we should 'change register' – and not only go beyond or take a further step 'beyond the line' – in relation to Heidegger's *narration* of the *Seinsgeschicte* (a 'history of being' governed by the oppositional pair oblivion/possibility of manifestation[33]), moving all its themes to a *logical-philosophical* level. Let me explain better. I think that what Heidegger calls 'the history of Nihilism and of metaphysics' is, in reality, a mannerist stylization that is entirely functional to an operation of self-legitimation. It is, of course, a philosophical self-legitimation *strictu sensu*; it is not trivially political-ideological, contrary to what Farias claims in his fretful pleading on 'Heidegger and Nazism'.[34] Yet, that self-legitimizing philosophical operation helps Heidegger towards his own self-positioning in a key moment of Western thought: the prelude to the new advent – or, as he used to say, the 'destiny' – of Being. As we know, the signature of this prelude would be represented in the global era dominated by the scientific-technological edifice (*Ge-Stell*), by Heidegger's thought itself, as it evolved – after the famous 'turn' – with the notion of ontological difference. Yet, precisely the problem of ontological difference – that assumes an incommensurable disparity between *being* and *entity* – is not a novelty introduced by Heidegger. Indeed, it had already been formulated in rigorous terms by the great Arabian and Jewish thought in Spain: suffice it to think of the theological *tawhīd* of Ibn'Arabi, with its distinction between *wojūd* and *mawjūd*, *esse* and *ens*, the level of the act-being and that of the 'entities', intended as the multiplicity of its 'manifestations' (for those who still nurture some doubts, I refer to the insightful diagnosis of the 'unconscious' Jewish heritage in Heidegger's thought, made by French scholar Marlène Zarader in *La dette impensée*[35] – in addition to the extraordinary pages devoted to this philosopher by Henry Corbin in *Le paradoxe du monothéisme*[36]). Once we understand that vague entity that we call 'history' as a *labyrinth*, and no longer as a *trajectory*, we can see the relevance of that logical-philosophical perspective for which radical questions are not located, once and for all, in a specific 'moment *x*' of the course of metaphysics and Nihilism; to the contrary, they periodically reappear within a non-linear dynamic, marked by exclusions and deletions, contrasts and repetitions: within a complex plot, then, that is substantially different from that suggested by a poorly hidden philosophy of history, in relation to the results of which, we, contemporaries, would be placed – simply and trivially – *after*.

Based on this, I would now like to illustrate briefly what I consider the conclusions of my work, which are, naturally, provisional. That is, I would like to present the consequences of what I have called *lateral shift*. These consequences are distributed on two levels, so to speak, which correspond to the *pars destruens* and *pars construens* of my reflection. I will then examine: first (a) *the aporia inherent in the concept of authentic time, as the 'actualization' of the past/ future pathology that is typical of ordinary time*; second (b) *the relation between the paradoxes of the experience of time and the 'disorientation' implicit in the space-time of post-relativistic science.*

8

The axis of time

The reductionism implicit in the criticism of chronological time, as proposed by the philosophies of authentic time, becomes apparent through a comparison with Aristotle, the author who is often chosen by the contemporary 'authenticity jargon' as the favorite target of its polemic. In my opinion, the Aristotelian consideration of the problem of time is still unsurpassed, precisely because it is grounded on an *aporetic procedure* (in the sense indicated above). As we saw at the beginning, Bergson's doctrine of *duration*, which centered on the antithesis of *temps-espace* and *temps-durée*, tried to overcome the classical concept of time by presenting it as unilateral. Yet, as Heidegger himself had understood, the whole of Bergson's conception 'rests on a misunderstanding of the Aristotelian interpretation'.[1] As a consequence, the concept opposed to that of 'ordinary time', i.e., duration, also proves untenable. This situation is particularly important if we consider the influence that Bergson's thought had on the images of the universe as proposed today by some important scholars of 'time's arrow', beginning with Prigogine. The misunderstanding relates to the interpretation of a key element of classical reflection, *number*. In particular, it relates to the misunderstanding engendered by the confusion between time that is *numbered* and time that is *measured, spatialized.*

The misunderstanding consists in reading Aristotle's famous definition of *chronos* – 'the numbering of motion according to before and after (*arithmòs kineseos katà to próteron kai hysteron*)'[2] – as a reduction of time to a simple measurement, mere quantity and calculability. In reality, when associating *arithmós* to *kínesis*, Aristotle meant to establish a biunivocal relation between 'time' and 'motion' – mathematicians would call it a 'bi-jective' relation – not an equivalence. This is an operation in which the most careful interpreters have even seen a brilliant anticipation of some of the themes of Einstein's physics.[3] Far from performing an objectivistic reduction of the question of time – as Bergson believed – Aristotle's reflection brings him to the *soul*. Reference to the *psyché* appears necessary, precisely because there is no objective link between time and motion, except for the intervention of the mind: of the 'subject' that thinks and re-elaborates the experience. The soul, the *psyche*, is then indispensable as the 'numberer' of time: 'we judge the more and the less according to a number, and the greater or lesser motion according to time: hence time is a number (*arithmòs ara tis ho chronos*). But because there are two ways of saying 'number' (for we call number not only the numbered and the numerable, but also the means by which we number), time is the numbered, and not the means by which we number. And the means by which we number and that which is numbered are two different things'.[4] In Aristotle, who practiced philosophy in a truly rigorous manner, consequences are cogently derived from the premises: if there is no numberer, there is no number, and if there is no number, there is neither numerable (*arithmetòn*) nor numbered (*arithmoúmenon*); therefore, *if there is no soul, there is no time*. But let us read this whole crucial passage:

> One could [...] wonder whether time would exist or not without the existence of the soul. For, if we do not admit the existence of the numberer, that of the numerable is also impossible so that, evidently, the number will not exist either (*adynatou gar ontos einai tou arithmésontos adynaton kai arithmetón ti einai, hosre delon hoti oud'arithmós*). Number is, indeed, either that which has been numbered (*to arithmemenon*) or that which is numerable (*to arithmetón*). But if it is true that, in the nature of things, only the soul and the intellect that is in the soul (*psyches noús*) are able to number, *then it is impossible that time exists without the soul*, unless we consider time in its subjectivity, the same way that, for example, we would admit the existence of motion without considering the soul.[5]

Faced with the logical consistency of this passage, it is truly difficult to imagine how Aristotle's discussion of time could have been understood as a kind of naïve objectivism by some twentieth century philosophers.

To link time to the soul – which is not the *anima mundi*, a cosmic soul of a stoic-(neo)platonic kind, but the human psyche – entailed, however, a radical shift of the entire question, in terms that will be reopened seven centuries later by Augustine. The thread linking book IV of the *Physics* to book XI of the *Confessions* has been nonchalantly ignored by that popular interpretive current of thought that superficially insisted on Augustine's 'Platonism' (in fact, a reference to Plotinus' III *Ennead* would be more appropriate here – but this is not the right place to delve into this). And when Edmund Husserl – in his lectures on the phenomenology of the 'inner awareness of time', given this century in Göttingen – referred to Augustine's 'unparalleled' reflection, he did not pronounce a single word on what the latter owed to the great Aristotelian diagnosis.[6]

Yet, the core elements of Augustine's conception of time were all anticipated in Aristotle. The idea that time, if it consisted of discrete instances would *dissolve into nothing*, was completely Aristotelian. 'One of its parts has been and is no longer, a part is about to be and is not yet' sounds like Augustine and yet, I am reading from book IV of the *Physics* ...[7]. If time is composed of parts, it dissolves into parts. Only the present moment then remains, which inexorably escapes us every time we try to seize it. Time, thus conceived, has *two arms that extend towards different directions of non-being*: the no-longer of the past and the not-yet of the future.

Herein lies the *aporia*, the dead end. There was only one way for Aristotle to get around it: to conceive of the 'present instant' (*now*) in a totally different way. But how?

The 'now', he says, must no longer be considered as a part, since it is not a limit (*peras*), but a number (*arithmós*). The boundaries of something, indeed, are one with the entity they demarcate. The same is not true of the number. Number is not constrained by what it numbers. It is characteristic of the number to be able to determine something without depending on the content or the way of being of the numbered. For example, when I say 'ten horses', the number ten demarcates the horses, while sharing nothing of their nature. It is not a limit of the horses as such, because with the same number I can determine other real entities (trees, ships) or mental ones (triangles). It is a characteristic of the number to determine something in such a way, that it remains independent from what it demarcates. When we say that *chronos* is the 'the numbering of motion according to before and after', therefore, we stress that we number and determine motion as 'passing' according to the 'now' (*nyn*); yet, this number is bound neither by the essential content of the 'moved' nor by motion as such.

The consequence of this conceptual operation is absolutely decisive: the 'now' is pulled away from the abstract, purely quantitative dimension of mathematics, and is included within the *continuum* of time – which is *both* objective and subjective, physical and psychical, emotional and mental. According to Aristotle, the 'now' – the temporal instant – is never a *limit* in itself (like a geometrical point), given that, as a *passage*, it is open towards the two sides of the not-yet and the no-longer. And yet . . .

And yet, this radical framing of the question of time poses more problems than it solves. It does so – I should add – not despite, but by virtue of its anticipating brilliance. It unveils, with a conceptual rigour that is *still unparalleled to date*, a pathological element deeply rooted in the Western experience of time: a pathology that has its clearest manifestation in the notion of *past future*.[8] Time – as revealed by Aristotle and developed by Augustine's doctrine of 'presentification' and Heidegger's theory of 'anticipation' – is a stream of 'nows' that move from the *now-not-yet* towards the *now-no-longer*: a flow that is not indeterminate, but that holds, in itself, a direction from the future towards the past.

It so happens that this 'presentifying' duration, taken by Augustine as the basis of the inner experience of time, contains a *drive towards expectation* that 'translates the future into the past'. The sentence recalled above is taken from a crucial, yet strangely ignored excerpt of the *Confessions*: in some sense, it marks the *logical-philosophical* conclusion (forgive me for the term) of the reflection on time in book XI (there is also, as we know, a *practical* conclusion, which solves the question of redemption and salvation – we will not go into it here, although it does endow the text with its unmistakable emotional character and tone). So, what does Augustine do in this excerpt? He does a beautiful thing: he ties the experience of time to the archetype of the *voice*. He says, then, implicitly: time can be measured either according to the revolving motion of stars – as in Plato – or according to the motion (and rest) of bodies – as in Aristotle; but there is an even more universal model for the measurement of time: the marking of voice intervals. In Augustine's scheme, as marvelously explained by Leo Spitzer, 'self-awareness is grounded on rhythmic-temporal elements: music, with its *durée réelle*, offers a field of research to inner senses that uniquely grasp the harmony of the universe and of God'.[9] All of the *De musica* seems permeated with the idea of a direct and intimate relation between the soul and the *Deus archimusicus*.[10] It is a representation that, according to Spitzer, can be understood only against the backdrop of the strong polarity between Augustine and Ambrosius:

> Contrary to Ambrose, who sees a host of choirs in the universe, Augustine reduces the human soul to a compact unity, and then derives from it the conscience of the monotheistic God.

> Before our eyes, rather than a theatre that embraces the whole world, there is a universal drama that proceeds to the end, invoking a 'sense of time' in the audience. We do not have here, as in Ambrose, an enlargement of the keyboard; it is the instrument of the soul that is spiritualized. The *Lied* that springs from Augustine's soul is linear and directly tends to God; it is closer to the solitary struggle with which the soul departs from the earth, as in a Beethovenian *largo*, than to the choral nature of baroque Jesuitical music.[11]

Thanks to this representation, we can include the concepts of interval and of pause in the 'numbering' of time: something very similar to the *temporal beat*. But it is precisely the example of the voice that leads Augustine to conclude that the endpoint of our experience of time – of our 'presentifying' re-elaboration of the events of time in the *trinitarian space of the present* (the present of the past, or memory; the present of the future, or expectation; the present of the present, or perception) – is a *becoming-future that tends to bend towards the past*. Let us then read the original version of the passage in question:

> Voluerit aliquis edere longiusculam vocem et constituerit praemeditando, quam longa futura sit, egit utique iste spatium temporis in silentio memoraeque commendas coepit edere illam vocem, quae sonat, donec ad propositum terminum perducatur; immo sonuit et sonabit; nam quod eius iam

> peractum est, utique sonuit, quod autem restat, sonabit atque ita peragitur, *dum praesens intentio futurum in praeteritum traicit diminutione futuri crescente praeterito, donec consumptione future sit totum praeteritum.* (Let us assume that someone wants to emit a slightly longer sound and has mentally established how long it will have to be: he has certainly covered in silence and consigned to memory that given lapse of time; he has, then, started to let out his voice, which plays until it reaches the established end; what's more, the voice that *has* played and *will* play: because what has already passed has undoubtedly played, and what remains of it will play. And this is how it passes, *while the present intention translates the future into the past, and the past grows while the future decreases, until, the future being eroded, all will be past*).[12]

What remains of Heidegger, then, and of his reflection on time? Well, *exactly the same thing* that we have just seen in Augustine happens in Heidegger – even if the terminology is for the most part different. It should be noted that – when observing the problem from our point of view – Heidegger's main ideas on time are not contained in his *Sein und Zeit,* which, as we know, ends with the second section of the first part. They are delivered during a course in the summer semester of 1927, devoted to the 'fundamental problems of phenomenology' (*Grundprobleme der Phänomenologie*), which he gives much later (in 1975), as a 're-elaboration of the third section of the first part of *Sein und Zeit*'[13] – in practice, the theoretical section of 'Time and Being', which had not been published with the 'historical' part of the book. In this course, Heidegger refers to the two reflections on time we considered here: Aristotle's and Augustine's. He treats all their dominant themes, but translates them into another vocabulary, which he considers finally in conformity with the 'original experience': Aristotle's *soul* becomes the *being-there* (*Da-sein*), that is, man's existence intended as being-in-the-world, while Augustine's *presentification* becomes *temporality* (*Zeitlichkeit*), intended as the condition for any experience of the 'events' of the world. Apart from the 'new' terminology – as already noted – the result is the same. Indeed, what does the *Zeitlichkeit* of the *Dasein*, the temporality of existence, consist in? It consists in a presentification tending to the future that is constantly pulled in a circle towards the past, so that the 'being-future' allows existence to 'repeat the past in the "how" (*Wie*) of its having-been-lived' and the "no-longer" becomes the 'authentic future'.[14] Practically speaking, Heidegger tells us that Augustine was right: we experience time by presentifying the sequence in the flow (the continuum) of duration; 'past' and 'future' are only ghosts capable of coming to life within the real duration of the present; and – therefore – all duration is, to use Husserl's words, an *epoché*, a pause, a 'halt', in which events are re-elaborated and put together. For this reason, Augustine is the author closest to the concept of 'original time'.[15] Except that the presentification can stop being captive of 'ordinary time' – of the instants-hour that inevitably pass dissolving into nothing – to the extent that the *being-there* is able to 'buy time' in forerunning the future, anticipating the event. But how is the event anticipated? Here we are helped by the Ariadne's thread of our journey. We can anticipate the event because we assimilate it to what is known, because we neutralize what is unforeseen and unsettling of the future by picturing it as similar to the past, to the events that we have already elaborated upon and put in the receptacle of our memory. The 'forerunning' is transformed into an extension of the memory's content.[16]

But, if authentic *temporality*, the 'how' of the being-each-time of the *Dasein*, consists in this endless short circuit between the anticipation of the not-yet and the no-longer, then our experience of time is always *off-axis* in relation to the present moment, i.e., – paradoxically – our experience of time is authentic to the extent that it is outside the time we actually live in (*The time is out of joint*, said poor Hamlet, *O cursed spite, That ever I was born to set it right*...). Heidegger betrays this paradox the moment in which he states that the dimension within which we experience time is 'ek-static'. 'Ecstatic', here, refers to nothing mystical. It only means that existence intimately deals with an *ek-statikón*, a 'destabilization'.[17] It means that it is an *ek-sistentia*, an *original outside-of-oneself*, a 'being-ecstatic' of the present that, from the forerunning of the future, is inexorably pulled back in circles towards the past: 'Original time is, in itself, outside itself – this is the essence of its temporalization. Time is this outside-of-oneself . . .'[18] The thread connecting the two most radical Western reflections on time, Aristotle's and Heidegger's – passing through the crossroads of Augustine's philosophy – demonstrates that our experience is dominated by a *hypertrophy of expectation*. Those who diagnose the 'pathology' of Modern man, such as Hans Jonas and Reinhart Koselleck, are right when they point to the *prematureness* grounding the symbolic dominance of the *waiting* and of a *planning tended towards the future*. We should be clear here: the pathology does not simply consist in the fact that there exists a form of time that tends to the future. This form is indeed present in all cultures, even if in different degrees: no civilization can avoid endowing itself with some measure of predictability, even if limited or minimal, the same way that it cannot entirely avoid repetition and cycles. The pathology does not lie in the fact of this presence, but in its *form* and *degree*. It is due to the fact that only *in the West* (to use an expression dear to Max Weber) has the anticipation of planning been singled out as an 'authentic' form, as a specific and dominant figure of the experience of time: Western men, said James Joyce, live as if every moment were the next one. For this reason, *precisely in the West*, 'normality' and 'ordinary' experience themselves take on the singular guises of a paradox. This *paradoxical status of normality*, which makes our *Zivilisation*, our 'civilization of technology', an exception compared to all other cultures (even if this exceptional character may appear less evident today, due to the global generalization of the Western forms of 'rationality') is not at all 'overcome', but simply transformed in Heidegger's notion of *Zeitlichkeit*, of original temporality.

From many sides, and rightly so, Western democracy is encouraged to take an anthropological perspective in the comparison of cultures.[19] The pathology of temporality enshrined in the figure of the past future is indeed nothing but a symbolic complex typical of our cultural context. This symbolic complex is rooted in that tendency to exorcise what is *foreign* and unknown, by assimilating it to what is familiar and known; a tendency that is present in all cultures. Yet, *only in the West* it has fully manifested itself as the *neutralization* of what is new, performed through the increasing *temporalization* of life forms: a neutralization of 'novelties' that – herein lies the paradox of the 'Modern' – *proceeds together with its stress on ideas and planning.*

Here Nietzsche goes further than Heidegger. I strongly believe – and this will certainly be a cause of debate for a significant part of contemporary philosophy – that there is not continuity, but a radical break between Nietzsche's and Heidegger's conceptions of 'Nihilism'. There is, in Nietzsche, an element that brings him close to Freud: the identification of that which estranges, that *disorientates* (a term that I prefer to 'perturbs', as a translation of

Un-heimlich), of the 'blind spot' of any perspective that tends to the future. Certainly, Heidegger's anticipation – related to project and existence – or 'ecstatic-horizontal temporality', as the condition of the ontological constitution of the Being-there, could be seen as the horizon-receptacle of the 'ordinary' experience of time, described as an irreversible sequence of 'nows'. But, precisely because of this, it is only, ultimately, its static interface. The same way that its ontology is nothing but the reverse side of the glove of ontic nomenclature: reversed reification, transfigured 'metaphysical horror'.[20]

All this explains, and is deeply related to, the serious manipulation of Nietzsche's concept of 'Nihilism', carried out by Heidegger in the years of the *Kehre*, and amply documented in the two volumes of the *Nietzsche* (1961). An analysis of this work – that is still largely ignored, particularly in the Italian 'debate'[21] – reveals the despotic seal that Heidegger put on the history of metaphysics and of Nihilism. It is the despotic seal of 'happening', whose ontological categories – let me repeat – are only the reverse side of the glove. Every thing that happens *must* happen, it cannot not happen. There is no redemption, just a prospective inversion of view point. Suffice it to look at things from the point of view of the *Ge-schick*, of the destination-destiny: perhaps trusting the fact that the delivery will keep on being made, that, in any case, the mailman always rings twice ... Before this dominance of 'destiny-governed' events, there is no longer the possibility to *question* what has happened. Heidegger's past is truly an endless no-longer: a past that does not pass, because it has already passed. But, on the other hand, it is also a past that does not change, that will never be able to be redeemed. In a brief conference on the concept of time (*Der Begriff der Zeit*), held in July 1924 before the Marburg Theologians, Heidegger gave the following, lapidary statement:

> In relation to death all men are led in a *uniform* way to the 'how' that they can be; to a possibility in relation to which no one is privileged; to the 'how' (*Wie*) in which every 'what' (*Was*) is *reduced to dust*.[22]

This is a literally *atrocious* statement, which casts a shadow of leaden darkness over the hidden meaning of authentic temporality. According to Heidegger, only the *levelling* of any particularity in the mode of death – the uniformity that erases all differences in advance – is truly authentic – that is, *eigentlich*, 'proper'. But is not anticipation the quintessence of original time? Does it not inexorably go back to the always-past, to the already-since-always-dead? And does this not inevitably derive from the premise that the set of 'possibles' is already all pre-determined by the *ek-static* horizontality of an '*ek-sistentia* that is constantly *off-axis* in relation to present life? Are there any alternatives for the past? There are, replies Heidegger. But only in the form of memorization, of a dead collection of plans. Certainly not in the

Benjaminian form of redemption, which is, above all, redemption of the dead: the only condition for changing the future.

At this point, I think it is necessary to refer to a cue contained in Freud's work: the obsession of expectation that, in the Western experience of time, continually surprises the present by neutralizing the 'new' and having it swallowed by a future that is constantly bent towards the past, has its pathological core in a *delayed sense of the event*. In the West, the seal of Sense is always destined to arrive *after*. That 'damned' philosopher who goes by the name of Hegel meant no defence of philosophy when he stated that Minerva's owl starts to fly when dusk falls. He just meant that philosophy always arrives when things are over, when the process has been brought to an end. In this sense, and in this sense *only*, he believed that philosophy, *his* philosophy, was the last word of Western history and thought. But why does all this happen? It does because, starting with Aristotle and following a path that ends precisely with Hegel, philosophy has no longer been in the *metaxý*, in tension. By sacrificing its *eros* on the altar of productive knowledge and historical action, it has wanted to escape tension; it has pretended to be 'its own time captured within thought'. Now you will say: what does Aristotle have to do with philosophy's own time captured within thought? Have you ever read the *Metaphysics*? It is a philosophy of history presented as a history of philosophy. Aristotle simply 'corrects' and 'overcomes' all that had come before him: the pre-Socratics, Socrates, Plato . . . then places his own thought as the apex and capstone of the entire process. This was exactly the blueprint, the model, of what Hegel would later do. It is this type of philosophy that had to end according to Schopenauer, Kierkegaard and Nietzsche. Instead, Heidegger re-proposes it, eliminating its dialectic, as well as the 'melancholy' and 'sad conscience' that permeated it, while imposing his despotic seal on the Nihilist parabola.

To sum up and conclude the discussion on this difficult and complex aspect: the tendency, started by Aristotle, to articulate the mystery of time *anthropomorphically*, hence to 'domesticate' it, legitimately belongs to the symbolic complex of the *past future*. Following Aristotle's line, from Augustine to Heidegger, the question '*what* is time?' becomes '*who* is time?'. And the answer was foregone from the beginning: we ourselves are time, *mea res agitur*. In this way, however, the philosophy of 'interiority', or of 'authenticity', has ended up exorcising that disorientating trait of the mystery that Plato's 'foreign gaze' had been able to establish, even if only briefly. It is not a coincidence that, today, the idea of *space-time* of post-Einsteinian science can refer to that gaze, to that 'perturbing' element.

9

Kairós and *tempus*

a. The mobile boundaries of language

Finally, we arrive at the *pars construens* of our *lateral shift*, which deals with the consequences for philosophical reflection of the paradoxes of time, as identified by the contemporary image of the physical world. Here, I do not intend – let me repeat – to refer to the frameworks formulated by the epistemologists of 'complexity' or by the theoreticians of Negentropy and of 'dissipative structures'. A few, brief notes are sufficient regarding the last two (while referring to my previous works for a deeper analysis). The paradigm formulated by the theoreticians of Negentropy is nothing but a stylization of the results of biological research, of a part of natural sciences that tends today towards an 'imperialist' attitude, even in the field of psychology (based on an extension of the models of *self-reference* and *self-observation*). My views might be distorted by a given 'professional attitude';

however, it is my impression that their notions of 'possibility' and of 'complexity' are not very 'perturbing' and are rather distant from the radicalness with which those same problems have been addressed by scholars like Leibniz (an author who, not by coincidence, has rapidly returned to the centre of contemporary reflection). As regards Prigogine and his 'dissipative structures', I believe that his notion of *time's arrow* is valid only upon one condition, which, however, itself rests on a very shallow foundation. All his theory is grounded on the hypothesis that that principle of asymmetry, that is, of temporal irreversibility (and of the relative 'negentropic' reversibility of open systems), which is valid for the *evolutionary residue* from which organized matter and living forms originate, can be extended to the whole universe.

At the source of these models, then, is the paradox that I highlighted in the most recent developments of my reflection (even if we admit their internal consistency, on which there is much to object; in fact, a lot has been objected by scientists of proven validity and rigour). It is the paradox pointed out recently by Thomas Gold,[1] one of the greatest cosmologists of our time: in our evolutionary residue, we experience a life and universe that are *asymmetrical* in relation to time, while all the laws that apply to them possess a *symmetry* that cannot be reconciled with the belief that time has an inherent quality that can be represented through the arrow metaphor (Eddington's famous *arrow of time*).

A legitimate doubt thus arises: that many of the present day epistemological frameworks hide, behind their stress on the 'discovery of time', a subtle neutralization of that unsettling element of contemporary scientific revolution (Einstein's relativity and quantum mechanics), which entails a *sacrificium intellectus sani*. Suffice it to think of the anthropomorphic appeal to common sense ('We all grow old together!') with which Prigogine, in his preface to the Italian edition of *De l'être au devenir*,[2] pretends to justify his own use of the arrow of time. It is no coincidence that Prigogine and Stengers are forced to consign Einstein to the captivity of the 'a-temporal model' of classical physics. Examining closer, we see that the *disorientating*, the 'untamable' element of relativity does not consist in time's 'irruption' into Newton's universe – as some might superficially be led to believe. To the contrary, it consists in the definitive incorporation of the temporal phenomenon into the curvature of space; of a space that has become a four-dimensional continuum. Time and change keep on existing, but – as W.V.O. Quine observed – incorporated in the four-dimensional multiplicity:

> When we view time in this perspective, a stable solid must be considered as if it extended into four dimensions: (1) above and below, (2) right and left, (3) front and back, (4) past and future. The system does not entail rejecting change in favor of an eternal stillness, as some have assumed: change is still

> there, with all its fresh surprises; simply, it is incorporated. [...] The *spatialization of time* helps logic in something more than simplicity and expediency. [...] In space, besides the directions 'above' and 'below', 'right' and 'left', 'front' and 'back', we also recognize all the intermediary oblique directions such as, for example, 'above to the left', 'down ahead': in sum, spatial dimensions can be mixed in any proportion. If the temporal dimension had to be completely subsumed under the old adequate threesome, so to allow us to freely deal with oblique directions such as 'above and then', 'ahead from now on', and so on, we would be forced to formulate equations between distance units and duration units: x number of miles equal one hour. In order to obtain the advantages we mentioned, such a total integration was unnecessary; it becomes necessary, however, in relativity theory.[3]

The *strong* implication of Einstein's relativity theory is not to state that 'space in itself is nothing' and 'time is nothing either',[4] as Heidegger thought (which says a lot about his scientific knowledge). It is embodied – as we saw previously – in a discovery so important that it constituted a blatant violation of common sense. It is important to recall, for one last time, the paradox that Einstein himself mentions in the *Autobiographisches*: it is true that, in the four-dimensional continuum of space-time, all that was absolute in Newton's system becomes relative; on the other hand, however, 'something' that was relative in Newton's universe becomes absolute. This something, this *quid*, is nothing less than light. With Einstein, natural light – with its constant speed, as already demonstrated by the famous experiment conducted by Michelson and Morley in 1888, eight years before a brilliant sixteen-year-old followed a ray of light to Zurich and jumped on it to see what would happen – suddenly becomes closer to Plotinus' intelligible light than to Newton's. Herein lies the *parádoxon* of relativity: in this glittering return of the *lumen divinum*, although in the guise of *lumen naturale*.[5] Faced with this *disorientation*, common sense stops: it is 'good' only for Newton's daily world, but it is useless for the shore-less ocean that demarcates it from the two sides of the infinitely large and infinitely small[6] – as Bohr's *quanta* and Heisenberg's *indeterminacy* will explain even more radically.

Our *evolutionary residue* and the daily experience that inhabits it, then, are plunged in a temporal dimension that is drawn into the paradoxes of *measurement* and *observation*, as revealed, respectively, by relativity theory and by quantum mechanics; paradoxes that are entirely typical of a universe that – whatever its forming principle, the *clinamen* of Bohr's 'chance' or the 'necessity' inscribed in the 'incomprehensible power' of the God of Einstein and Newton – seems to take on a hologram-like structure, in which all things seem to be held mysteriously, and in which each part (as understood in the brilliant anticipations of Lullo and Leibniz, Bruno and Spinoza) seems to have all the information of the whole in itself. Yet, our mind cannot grasp the cipher of this hologram actually, nor, perhaps, even potentially.

To redefine experience starting from this indeterminate depth of perspective, from this disorientating *adverse background* of Reason and Logos, means to re-think our existence in the universe in light of a *radical idea of the limit*. Herein lies the fundamental problem. Philosophy, particularly modern – despite the strenuous efforts of Hume and Kant – has never been able to *inform (educare)* the rational project *with the limit*. It seems to me, instead, that psychoanalysis can help philosophy in this matter. To *e-ducate* means, literally, to take the 'Subject' out from the mobile cage of the Consciousness and the Super-Ego, so that it may lean over the boundary lines, the borders that demarcate and constitute it. It means to acquire the sense of that rigorous distinction (and decision) that alone allows us to force or doubt the limits of 'rationality', but also, at the same time, to give our formal languages the consistency that can only derive from the awareness that language is not everything. Stated otherwise, it is possible to force the boundaries, on the condition that we recognize them as such; and, conversely, it is possible to formalize what can be said, on the condition that we know that everything cannot be said. Wittgenstein's 'silence' itself, the *Schweigen* which closes the *Tractatus*, is not the abyss of silence that precedes and surrounds the language-world, but a *paradoxical word*; it is a word that comes *after language*, after we have experienced completely the expressive potential of all words.

In order to illustrate the 'positive' implications of what I mean by lateral shift, I would now like to point to *two articulations of the limit* in which it is possible to formulate an 'off-axis' approach to the question of time.

b.1. The realm of experience

The *first articulation of the limit* is strictly linked to one of the dominant themes of my book: the need for a *rehabilitation of space*. This rehabilitation – it helps to repeat – is not restorative in character; it does not nostalgically hint at any metaphysics of space. Instead, it tries to point to an *impossibility theorem*. The presumed innocence of inner awareness, by virtue of which we would grasp time in its purity and authenticity, dissolves as soon as we face the *aporia* of the image and the representation – as 'good old' Einstein had well understood. Every time we try to perceive time 'live', we realize that we can comprehend no event unless we put it in a context. No perception of becoming is innocent, because no perception can do without an original structure that affects it and contaminates it spatially. There is, then, an original *symbolic* space, presupposed to measurement itself, that prejudges *a priori* any pretense of 'authenticity'. 'If, among all words, there is an inauthentic one', once observed Maurice Blanchot, 'it is certainly the word "authentic"'. Here, I must refer to some *Leitmotive* of my previous works. How could we experience the events of our life, if we did not put them within a context, not only in our memory or expectation, but also in the moment in which they occur? Were we not able to 'dream' them – not only when asleep, but also when awake? Doesn't that great initial (and initiating) text of the twentieth century, the *Traumdeutung*, teach us precisely that dreams are an original *mise-en-scène*, which is antecedent to the constitution of identity itself, to the very distinction between the 'subject' and the 'object' of knowledge? If we stop and think for one moment, the *revolutionary* content of the 'off-axis' perspective cannot end with the identification of the original ('pre-categorical' and 'intransitive') *affective character* of the experience (*Erlebnis*) of time[7]. It cannot, for the simple but decisive reason that the juxtaposition of 'emotional' and 'rational', or also of 'emotional' (*pathos*) and 'semantic' (*semainómenon*), cannot assign the whole realm of representation to the second term. This realm, indeed, touches not only on the *Bewusst* of 'awareness', but also on the *Un-bewusst*, the unconscious of 'dreams'.

The disorientation evoked by the off-axis perspective consists precisely in this, in taking as the horizon (and not the Presupposition!) of all our experiences of the world an *oneiric virtual element* that circumscribes and includes in itself the two dimensions of wake and sleep, of the diurnal and the nocturnal realms. Through this path, I have tried to relate to Wilfred R. Bion's notion of 'contact barrier', which was brilliantly anticipated in one of the opening sentences of Edgar Allan Poe's short story *Eleanor*: 'Those who dream by day are cognizant of many things which escape those who dream only by night.' In Bion's revision of Freud's 'subconscious' the juxtaposition between 'diurnal' and 'nocturnal' is dissolved in a continuum. Dreams keep the privileged position they were ascribed by Freud, but end up playing a different, somehow more complex, role. In the *Traumdeutung*, as we know, dreams were the distorted representation of an already present unconscious meaning. Which means that Freud, as a 'master of doubt', had not developed a theory of the *construction* of meaning, but of its *disguise*. Conversely, Bion considers dreams an attempt to create a new meaning starting from a *pathos*, an 'attachment', an emotional experience. Given that it is not possible, for obvious reasons, to delve into the details of the most technical aspects of Bion's theory, I will limit myself to some essential observations. In Bion, the juxtaposition between sleep and wake (or awareness) is replaced with the pair alpha function/beta function; the former, by acting on the sensations and emotions of experience, produces some 'elements', or 'memories', which become operational both in sleep and wake; the latter represents the experience of the same facts as 'objects', 'things', 'non-thoughts'.[8] *Consciousness* and *unconsciousness*, then, are both the product of a distinction made by the alpha function; in turn, this distinction constitutes the contact barrier, (or 'alpha screen'). Stated otherwise, *Bewusst* and *Unbewusst* cease to be two psychic regions – as in the first Freudian thought – and become 'transitional and reversible states of the mental experience'.[9] Thanks to the contact barrier, the oneiric dimension becomes an integral part of thought in the waking state: 'every man', writes Bion, 'should be able to "dream" of an experience while it happens to him, whether this occurs when he sleeps or when he is awake'.[10] The consistent development of this theory entails, as a decisive consequence, the inversion of the relationship between dreaming and unconsciousness: *it is not unconsciousness that produces the dream but, conversely, it is the 'act of dreaming' that creates, at the same time, unconsciousness and consciousness.*

b.2. 'Due' time

The *second articulation of the limit* is linked to the need for a new understanding of the evolutionary residue of our universe, within which living forms and our existence in the world find their 'due' time. How should we intend 'due *time*'? What is exactly 'our' time, what is the '*appropriateness*' of time? What is its dimension in relation to the spatial-temporal *disorientation* that constitutes and dominates it? In order to answer these questions, it is necessary to reflect again on language, examining a peculiar fact of Indo-European vocabulary, underpinning which is a question that is, at this point, decisive: the mystery of the origins of the Latin word *tempus*.

Few have reflected on the fact that the [Italian, *translator's note*] word 'tempo' – derived from the Latin *tempus* – replaces, in romance languages, the two words that indicate, in English and German, chronological time and meteorological time: *time* and *weather*, *Zeit* and *Wetter*. A curious fact is that the etymology of this key word is uncertain. For a long time, it was believed that it was a noun deriving from two Greek verbs: *teino*, which means to tend, to extend, to stretch; and *temno*, which means to cut. Both hypotheses seemed to refer to plausible meanings: time as extension and *continuity*, and time as cut, rhythm, *discontinuity*. This double etymology, however, is incorrect. While investigating the mysterious origins of the Latin word *tempus*, I have stumbled upon an essay by Emile Benveniste, in which, I think, there is a possible solution. Benveniste's argument (formulated back in 1940,[11] but *almost* never considered by 'professional philosophers'[12]) is the following: the difficulty in finding the etymology of *tempus* is due to the fact that the compounds of this word are, in reality, older than the word 'tempo' itself and, therefore, bear much more ancient traces than *tempus* does. The noun *tempus*, then, was born as an abstract derivation of terms such as *tempestus, tempestas, temperare* and, therefore, *temperatura*, *temperatio*, etc. The word tempus, surprisingly, would indicate the wisdom inscribed in the genetic code of a language that was able to employ one word for two phenomena, which we ended up considering distant if not even heterogeneous. It is as if the unitary nature of the term indicated the awareness that what we call 'tempo' is nothing but the interface of different elements, from which the reality of evolution derives; a 'mixture' (does not 'to cut' also mean 'to mix'?) that makes tempus something very close to what the Greek used to call *kairós*: *due time*, *appropriate time*.

The implications of this argument can blaze new paths from a strictly philosophical point of view: the Greek correlative of *tempus* is not *chronos*, but *kairós*. Distancing himself from other etymological hypothesis, Benveniste relates the word *kairós* (deriving from the Indo-European roots **krr*-) to the meaning of the verb *keránnymi*, 'to mix', 'to temper', reaching the conclusion that 'tempus corresponds, in its different meanings, to *kairós*'.[13] Far from the meaning of 'momentary instant', or 'opportunity' – which was a typical proto-modern understanding of the term[14] – *kairós* comes to designate, like *tempus*, a very complex figure of temporality, which recalls the 'quality of conformity' and the *proper mixture* of different elements exactly like the notion of *weather*.[15] In its spatial version, in fact, the same word indicates the proper sites, the vital parts of an organism 'in shape', that is, balanced and tempered in its components.[16]

Perhaps, precisely the idea of *tempus-kairós*, of the proper time of 'equilibrium', of the 'appropriate mixture',[17] is able to reinstate the sense of our evolutionary residue and, with it, of our very existence. But there is more. The figure of the *residue* forces us to reassess, in a different light, not only the relation between *tempus* and its Greek 'twin', but also that between the word *tempus* and its Latin alter-ego *spatium*. *Spatium* is indeed a compound, not a simple word. It derives from the root *pat-* and, therefore, it is related to the verb *pateo, patere*, which means 'to be open', 'evident' (hence the Italian adjective 'patente' = 'manifest'). Now, the 's', in *s-patium*, works as a prefix, a profoundly incisive and separating one: as in *se-cernere* (to emit), *se-parare* (to separate), *se-lectio* (selection), etc. The term, then, contains a reference to the sense of 'residue' in terms of an opening up. Significantly, in light of these etymological considerations, Carl Schmitt (another author that was not at all reductive towards the Latin linguistic heritage, unlike Heidegger) decided to liquidate the word *spatium* as a hostile and 'inhabitable' one, to which he opposed the 'mystical strength of the original German word *Raum*'.[18] In my perspective, instead, the word *spatium* acquires a decisive relevance, for the same reasons that led Schmitt to discard it. The relevance lies in the paradoxical role playing that it performs with *tempus*. By virtue of this role playing, *tempus*, as the 'balanced composition', the union of elements, becomes the relation and 'housing structure' of life forms, while *spatium*, as a residue, indicates the constitutive uncertainty and instability of any 'dwelling'. Taken together, the two words seem to express – admirably, without upsetting those longing to hold on to the expression 'to inhabit' – a spontaneous philosophy that is far more ironic and deep than that of many 'philosophers'. Significantly, indeed, the theme of the inevitable nature of 'time' as the complex dimension, the climatic configuration of existence, is more common in some great poetic texts (also Anglo-Saxon ones) than in philosophical works.[19] Perhaps it is here, in the wisdom that permeates the Latin language, that we should seek the profound reason for which the Romans never felt the need for a Philosophy.

Our time – ancient wisdom tells us today – is the time of living forms, of the world that evolves, precisely because it is originally ingratiated by the *kairós*. We can only experience the dimension of due time, of 'kairological' time, independently from the nature of the *disorientation* that delimits it, whether *kairós* comes after Bohr's and Heisenberg's 'indeterminacy' or whether it originates from Newton's and Einstein's 'incomprehensible power' – for which there is a plan of the 'Great Old Man' and 'God does not play dice'.[20]

It is useless to underline the closeness of this theme with others that go well beyond philosophy, and that were anticipated in Judaism. I believe that Freud's *Unheimlich* also has its remote roots here: in the idea of a destiny that looks at us from afar, pushing us to find, beyond any idol or fetish, the measure of our *kairós*, our due time. At this point, the multiple 'being-oneself' (that many talk about today) will unfold, but against the backdrop of the 'perturbation'. I think this is how Valéry portrayed the problem when he noted in his *Cahiers*:

> We call 'We ourselves' the need that we feel to relate any thing to one only *object* that is always the *same*. If we perceived the real variation of this *object* – which must necessarily change – we would no longer have the *I*. But all unfolds *as if* it were unchangeable. For this reason, it is sufficient that the changes of the perceived thing and those of the *perceiver* are equal and corresponding. We can then say that the *I* is the *equation* of those changes. We can then see that the most important thing is this *duality*. But the equation fluctuates. *The I is only roughly constant* – it is *I* only roughly.[21]

Thus intended, the *modular I* is not the playful expression, the multilateral life that we are euphorically told by that thick legion of postmodern philosophers and epistemologists. It is a serious 'placing our bets', to the extent to which we can place them. It is a serious forcing of the limits, after having rigorously articulated them.

I think this is the only lesson that philosophy – a philosophy that finally returned to its place of origin, to its *metaxý* – can give to life … starting from the lucid awareness that death remains the blind spot of the self-representation of any 'living thing', any 'identity': a death that does not stand before the course of life as its conclusion or interruption, but that stands behind it. Death is what has been removed from 'time' – time as *chronos*, the time of devoured moments. Because death is nothing but *waiting for a conclusion*: immobile waiting for a last instant that is both cruelly defined and cruelly imminent. It is necessary to correct and radicalize in this sense Freud's thought on the problem of death: we can hold the 'foreign gaze' of Death if we realize that death arrives not when we die, when the *I* dies, but in the very moment in which the *I* says 'I'. Precisely because death starts from that 'residue' of the infinite indetermination of the sense we call Identity. As soon as I say 'I', I have constituted myself starting from death – from *my* death.

Why, then, are we so afraid of it?

Maybe because we cannot make it ours. Because it is a 'future' devoid of any possible 'anticipation' (Levinas).[22] Because no *I*, no identity can truly 'understand' its own death in the mode of thinking that has been dominating to date. The mode of the *proprium*, of property, appropriation. As something completely Other, only death gives us the code of any possible 'being-other', starting from that of the 'friend' that Augustine already considered incommensurable: distant closeness, irreducible to any *measure*, any 'possessive' measurement unit of the Subject.

Due time, then, refers to this Other. *Due*: what is due, the gift, the inclusive and binding responsibility of time. Of a time that is not 'appropriate', authentic, because it can never be truly and only 'mine': because, paradoxically, it is always the Other that makes it possible for me.

In the reality (and hyper-realities) we happen to live in, we all experience the problem of ontology to the extreme of its manifestation. Our daily experience is no longer naively basic or vacuous, but is permeated with the symbols, images and metaphors transmitted by science and art: languages that constantly suspend and re-elaborate the experience of the limit, turning it more and more into an *extreme experience*.[23] It is about time that philosophy acknowledges it. If it does not want to be reduced to playing a residual role, or dissolving into other 'practices', it will have to learn how to regain the only *dýnamis* with which it was endowed by the 'demon' from the beginning: the role of a *powerful hermeneutic*, placed within the tension of the *metaxý* – in the *passage* between life and knowledge, experience and truth, 'limit' and 'unknown', but also in the persisting *interim* between wandering and dwelling, exile and kingdom, desperation and hope. In a time of *cosmic disorientation*, *philo-sophèin* can mean nothing but to stubbornly repeat this *interlude*.

Nec sine te nec tecum vivere possum . . .

NOTES

Preface to the English Edition (2024)

1 Hartmut Rosa, *Beschleinigung*, Suhrkamp, Frankfurt am Main 2005.

2 Carlo Rovelli, 'Forget time'. *Found Phys* 41, (2011), p. 1475.

Preface to the New Italian Edition (2020)

1 On the Lysippean representation of Kairós see the works of P. Moreno, *Testimonianze per la teoria artistica di Lisippo*, Canova, Treviso 1973; Kairós, in 'Enciclopedia dell'Arte Antica', IV, Treccani, Rome 1995, p. 289; Lisippo, *L'arte e la fortuna,* Fabbri, Milan 1995; *L'attimo fuggente*, in 'Archeo magazine', XXII, 10, 260, October 2006, pp. 114 ff.

2 For a genealogy of the meanings of the term from the Homeric age to classical Greece, see M. Trédé, *Kairós: l'à-propos et l'occasion. Le mot et la notion d'Homère à la fin du IVe siècle avant J.C.*, Klincksieck, Paris 1992.

3 See E. Panofsky, *Il Padre Tempo*, in Id., *Studi di iconologia*, Einaudi, Turin 1975, pp. 89 ff. For an analysis of the figural typology of the 'Father Time' I refer to my book *Potere e secolarizzazione. Le categorie del tempo*, Editori Riuniti, Rome, 1983, new expanded edition, Bollati Boringhieri, Turin 2005, pp. 50 ff.

4 However, see for this G. Polizzi, *Tempo e pensiero topologico tra scienze e filosofia. Intorno alla riflessione sulla miscela e sul kairós in Serres e in Marramao* in Id., *Tra Bachelard e Serres. Aspetti dell'epistemologia francese del Novecento*, Siciliano Editore, Messina 2003, pp. 223–258.

5 On the subject of musical rhythm, it is worth recalling Adorno's famous definition of *kairós*: suspended time that encompasses the anticipation and anamnesis of an entire musical journey (cf. T.W. Adorno, *Il fido maestro sostituto*, Einaudi, Turin 1969, p. 263).

6 See H. Weinrich, *Il tempo stringe. Arte ed economia della vita a termine*, Il Mulino, Bologna 2006, p. 242 and note; English: *On Borrowed Time*, translated by Steven Rendall, The University of Chicago Press, Chicago and London 2008, p. 230: "On the unresolved problem of the etymology of the word *tempus*, see Giacomo Marramao: 'We must reflect once again on language, taking as our example . . . the mystery of the origin of the Latin word *tempus*'". But by Weinrich see also, from a strictly linguistic point of view, the classic work of 1966, *Tempus. La funzione dei tempi nel testo*, il Mulino, Bologna 1978.

7 É. Benveniste, *Latin tempus*, in *Mélanges de philologie, de littérature et d'histoire anciennes offerts à Alfred Ernout*, Klincksieck, Paris 1940, p. 13.

8 The ambivalence of *kairós* is at one with the ancipital profile of contingency. This crucial node has been brought into focus with impeccable lucidity by Roland Barthes: on the one hand, *kairós* represents the instant of decision, the 'stroke of genius', the 'moment in its pure state of exception'; on the other hand, it represents the 'right moment' to be seized as a precarious, 'fragile' and 'perishable' conjuncture. See R. Barthes, *Le Neutre. Cours et seminaires au Collège de France (1977–1978)*, Seuil, Paris 2002, pp. 214 ff; partial translation in *Kronos e Kairos*, edited by Lorenzo Benedetti (with essays by Roland Barthes, Giacomo Marramao, Giovanni Gurisatti), Mondadori-Electa, Milan 2019, pp. 37 ff.

9 The theme of acceleration can be found, in close dialogue with Koselleck, since the first edition (1983) of my book *Potere e secolarizzazione*, cit. For the syndrome of haste I refer instead to another of my texts: *La passione del presente. Breve lessico della modernità-mondo*, Bollati Boringhieri, Torino 2008.

10 For these aspects, I refer to my *Passaggio a Occidente. Filosofia e globalizzazione*, new edition, Bollati Boringhieri, Turin, 2009 and to the English edition, further enlarged, *The Passage West*, Verso, London and New York 2012 – about which see also the international discussion translated and collected in the volume *Filosofia dei mondi globali. Conversazioni con Giacomo Marramao*, edited by Stefano Franchi and Manuela Marchesini, Bollati Boringhieri, Turin 2017 (with contributions by Peter Baker, Martin Jay, Andy Lantz, Alberto Moreiras, Pedro Ángel Palou, Carlos Rodriguez, Teresa M. Vilarós and Hayden White).

Chapter 1

1 I. Newton, *Mathematical Principles of Natural Philosophy*, Italian edition, *Opere*, I, Turin 1965, pp. 105–106 (emphasis added).

2 J. T. Fraser, *Time: The Familiar Stranger*, Amherst MA, 1987; Italian translation, p. 224

3 Newton, (n 1) p. 793 (emphasis added).

4 G. W. Leibniz, *Philosophical Papers and Letters*. Italian edition, *Saggi filosofici e lettere*, translated and edited by Vittorio Mathieu, Laterza, Bari, 1963, p. 391.

5 See G. W. Leibniz, 'De rerum originatione radicali', in *Die philosophischen Schriften* Gottingen, VII, p. 301.

6 Leibniz (n 4) pp. 400–401.

7 See H. Bergson, *Essai sue les données immédiates de la conscience*. Italian edition, Turin, 1964, pp. 125ff.

8 See H. Bergson, *La pensée et le mouvant*, in *Œuvres*, Paris, 1963, p. 1271.

Chapter 2

1 J. T. Fraser, *The Familiar Stranger*, Amherst MA, 1987, p. 42.

2 H. Bergson, *Essai sur les données immédiates de la conscience.* Italian edition, *Saggio sui dati immediati della coscienza*, translated by Gisèle Bartoli, Boringhieri, Turin, 1964, pp. 220.

3 A similar incorrect interpretation of Plato's work can be found in Fraser himself: see n 1, pp. 37, 40.

4 *Eikò … kinetón tina aionos: Timaeus* 37d 5–6. For a history of the term (and its meaning in Plato) see H. Willms, *EIKON. Eine begriffsgeschichtliche Untersuchung zum Platonismus*, Bd. I, Münster 1935.

5 The connection *aión-psyché* is clearly present in the *Iliad* (*epèi de ton ge lipe psyche te kai aión: Il.* 16, 453). See P. Chantraine, *Dictionnaire étymologique de la langue grecque: histoire des mots*, I, Paris 1968, pp. 42a–42b.

6 Homer, *Il.* 19, 27. The discovery of the meaning of *aión* as 'vital force' had led to radical revisions of a famous definition by Wilamowitz, for which—starting with Homer—*aión* would indicate time in a *relative* sense, while *chronos* would be time in an *absolute* sense: '*aión* ist die Zeit relative, während *chronos* dieselbe absolut ist' (U. Wilamowitz-Möllendorf, *Euripides: Herakles*, Berlin 1909, p. 363). This argument seems to be based on Aristotle's definition of *aión* as *periechon*, that is, as 'the last term (*telos*) that limits the time (*chronos*) of each life' (*to telos to periechon ton tes ekastou zoés chronon, De Cael.* 279 a 25). On the persistence of the meaning of *aión* as 'life' in Plato himself (e.g., in *Gorgia*, 448 c 6, or in the *Laws*, III, 701 c 4), see E. des Places, '*Lexique de la langue philosophique et religieuse de Platon*', in Platon, *Oeuvres completes*, XVI/1, Paris, 1964, p. 20.

7 E. Benveniste, '*Expression indo-européenne de l'éternité*', in *Bulletin de la Société de Linguistique*, XXXVIII, Paris 1937, p. 105. On the relationship between *aión* and *aevum* (that we will treat below), and the hypothesis of their common derivation from the form *ayu-*, see A. Ernout-A. Meillet, *Dictionnaire étymologique de la langue latine. Histoire des mots*, Paris 1932, p. 20. Here, *aevum* is defined as the '"time" considered in its duration, as opposed to *tempus*, which indicates […] a punctual element of duration'. Precisely in relation to this definition of *tempus*, as we will show in the last chapter, Benveniste clearly distances himself from the

Ernout-Meillet dictionary, which, nevertheless, is one of the main sources of his work.

8 Ibid., p. 104. The connection with *ayuh* in Sanskrit was already present in E. Boisacq, *Dictionnaire étymologique de la langue grecque, étudiée dans ses rapports avec les autres langues indo-européennes*, Heidelberg-Paris 1923, p. 31. See also P. Chantraine, *La formation des noms en grec ancien*, Paris 1933, p. 166. For an iconography of Aión, see D. Levi, *Aión*, in 'Hesperia', XIII (1944), pp. 269ff.

9 A.J. Festugière, '*Le sens philosophique du mot aión*', in *La parola del passato*, IV (1949), pp. 172–89.

10 Proclus, *In Plat. Remp.* 17, 10 Kroll. According to others, the 'genealogic inversion' remains 'unsolved and problematic' and it finds its plastic representation in the personifications of the two words as performed, respectively, by Euripides and Proclus: while, for Euripides, Aión is the son of Chronos (Heraclid. 900), Proclus states exactly the reverse – as we just mentioned. On this point, see E. Degani, *AIÓN. Da Omero ad Aristotele*. Padua 1961, p. 83.

11 Diels-Kranz 31B16.

12 *Timaeus*, 37 d 2-7.

13 See F. M. Cornford, *Plato's Cosmology*, London, 1937, particularly p. 98; J. Whittaker, 'The Eternity of the Platonic Form', in *Phronesis, XIII* 1968, pp. 131ff. For an accurate overview of these interpretations, see Franco Ferrari's foreword to the recent Italian edition of *Ennead*. III, 7: Plotinus, *L'eternità e il tempo*, with introduction by M. Vegetti, Milano 1991.

14 Degani, (n 10) p. 81. According to Philippson (*Origini e forme del mito greco*, Turin 1949, pp. 2ff.), in the intensity of its *nyn*, Plato's *aión* would be close to Parmenides' definition of Being. But, as a point with no dimensions, it would also recall the epiphanic time of the event, expressed by the *exaíphnes* (the 'instantaneous') of *Parm.* 156 d–e. On this point, see G. Marramao, *Minima temporalia. Tempo, spazio, esperienza*, Milano 1990, p. 131 (new edn, Bollati Boringhieri, Torino 2022).

15 According to Pierre Chantraine (*Dictionnaire étymologique de la langue grecque*, IV/2, Paris 1980, pp. 1277b–78a) the etymology of *chronos* is still uncertain; while both in Boisacq (n 8) pp. 1071–1072 and in the more recent H. Frisk (*Griechisches etymologisches Wörterbuch*, II, Heidelberg 1970, p. 1122) we find a – cautious – reference to the Indo-European root **gher-*. In addition, Frisk considers unlikely the hypothesis made by E. R. Curtius – which poses a link with *chortos*, giving *chronos* the meaning of 'umfassende Zeitgrenze'.

16 Van Windekens' argument is also mentioned in Frisk, ibid.

17 *Tim.* 37 d 5-8.

18 Therefore, I consider misleading Enzo Degani's argument, according to which Proclus' neo-Platonism, 'while distancing itself from the *Timeus*, simply develops, in practice, the Platonic premises, given that the anteriority and superiority of eternity in relation to time were already implicit in Plato, and the existence of *chronos* itself necessarily presumed the *aión*' (ibid., p. 84).

19 See *Ennead.* III 7.13, 19–30. Concerning the fundamental problem of the relationship between *chronos* and *aión*, I believe there is a point of convergence between my reflection and that carried out by Massimo Cacciari in *Dell'Inizio,* Adelphi, Milano, 1990, pp. 235ff. Beyond this point, however, it is my impression that our paths diverge. It is just a feeling, given that, in philosophy, 'walking a path' always means to mark a step in situ.

Chapter 3

1 I. Prigogine and I. Stengers, *Entre le temps et l'étérnité*. Italian edition, *Tra il tempo e l'eternità*, Bollati Boringhieri, Turin 1989, p. 33.

2 P. Coveney and R. Highfield, *The Arrow of Time*. Italian edition, *La freccia del tempo,* Rizzoli, Milan 1991, pp. 17–18.

3 Ibid., p. 119.

4 A. Einstein, '*Autobiografia scientifica*', in E. Bellone (ed.), *Opere scelte,* Turin 1988, p. 75 (emphasis added).

5 For a brief but rigorous clarification of this question, see E. Garin, '*Einstein filosofo*', in E. Garin and L. Radicati di Brozolo, *Considerazioni su Einstein*, Istituto Italiano per gli Studi Filosofici, Naples 1989, particularly pp. 12ff.

6 M. Schlick, *Space and Time in Contemporary Physics*. Italian edition, *Spazio e tempo nella fisica* contemporanea, with preface by L. Geymonat, Bibliopolis, Naples 1979, p. 95.

7 See Einstein, (n 4), p. 86.

8 The excerpt is taken from Garin (n 5) p. 9.

9 Einstein, (n 4), pp. 85–86 (emphasis added).

10 Ibid., p. 86.

11 Ibid.

12 Ibid., p. 63.

13 Ibid.

14 Ibid., pp. 63–64.

15 Ibid., p. 64.

16 A. Païs, 'Subtle is the Lord . . .'. *The Science and the Life of Albert Einstein*, Oxford 1982, p. 5.

17 Einstein, (n 4) p. 64.

18 Ibid.

19 Ibid.

20 Ibid.

21 S.W. Hawking and W. Israel (eds), *300 Years of Gravitation*, Cambridge 1989, p. 651.

22 The excerpt, drawn from a conversation of June 1989, is quoted by Coveney and Highfield themselves, (n 2), p. 112.

23 On this point, see Païs, (n 16), ch. 26 (devoted to the relationship between relativity theory and quantum mechanics). See also

W. Heisenberg, 'The Development of the Interpretation of the Quantum Theory', in W. Pauli (ed.), *Niels Bohr and the Development of Physics*, London 1955, pp. 12–29. For Roger Penrose's position on relativity, refer to his essay 'Singularities and Time-Asymmetry', in Hawking and W. Israel (eds), *General Relativity. An Einstein Centenary Survey*, Cambridge 1979.

Chapter 4

1 With this first delimitation of field, and in the middle of his important book *The Emperor's New Mind*, Oxford 1989, Penrose begins the treatment of what he calls the quantic 'magic' and 'mystery' (see, more generally, Chapter 6). The relevance of the considerations of the Oxford physicist-mathematician is not only scientific, and not even only 'epistemological' but, above all – as I will try to show in these pages – philosophical. The chapter opens with the question: 'Do philosophers need quantum theory?' Unless otherwise indicated, all the quotations made in this section are drawn from the above-mentioned work (now available also in an Italian edition, *La mente nuova dell'imperatore*, translated by L. Sosio, Rizzoli Milan 1992).

2 See E. Schrödinger, '*Die gegenwärtige Situation in der Quantenmechanik*', in *Naturwissenschaften*, XXIII (1935), pp. 807ff; more generally, see Schrödinger's, *Scienza e umanesimo. Che cos'é la vita?*, Florence 1970, pp. 68ff. and 183ff.

3 See R. Penrose, 'Quantum Physics and Conscious Thought', in B. J. Hiley and F. D. Peat (eds), *Quantum Implications: Essays in Honour of David Bohm*, London and New York 1987.

4 On the *aesthetic* relevance of the truth criterion in mathematical models, see R. Penrose, 'The Role of Aesthetics in Pure and Applied Mathematical Research', in *Bulletin of the Institute of Mathematics and Its Applications*', X (1974), 7/8, pp. 266–71.

5 G. De Santillana and H. von Dechend, *Hamlet's Mill.* Italian edition, *Il mulino di Amleto*, translated and edited by Alessandro Passi, Adelphi, Milan 1983.

6 Ibid., pp. 391–392.

7 See R. Penrose, 'Einstein's Vision and the Mathematics of the Natural World', in *The Sciences*, March 1979, pp. 6–9.

Chapter 5

1 See E. Husserl, *Ideen zu einer reinen Phänomenologie und phänomenologischen Philosophie*, I, Den Haag 1950, § 86.

2 On this point, see K. Pomian, *L'ordre du temps*, Paris 1984; as well as the discussion on this book by P. Rossi in *Il passato, la memoria, l'oblio*, Bologna 1991, pp. 119ff.

3 J. T. Fraser, *The Familiar Stranger*, Amherst MA, 1987; Italian edition, p. 111.

4 Ibid., pp. 182–183.

Chapter 6

1 On this point, see R. Bodei, *Erfahrung/Erlebnis. Esperienza come viaggio, esperienza come vita*, in V.E. Russo (ed.), *La questione dell'esperienza*, Florence 1991, pp. 114–24.

2 For this aspect, I refer to Aldo Masullo's essay, '*Sulla questione del "tempo"*' in *Iride*, 1991, 6, p. 193. In discussing analytically my previous publications on this theme, Masullo refers to, and develops, some important themes of his recent reflection, which I will treat below.

3 *Familiar stranger*, the original subtitle of Fraser's book, already mentioned above, is a Freudian-like expression, which, I believe, renders well the correct meaning of 'das Unheimliche' as 'heimliche Unheimlichkeit'.

4 See *Symposium* 202 a 2-3; 202 d 11.

5 *Symp.* 202 d 13-202 and 1.

6 *Symp.* 204 a 1-2.

7 *Symp.* 202 and 2-4.

8 K. Jaspers, *The Origin and Goal of History*. Italian edition, *Origine e senso della storia*, translated by Amerigo Guadagnin, Edizioni di Comunità, Milan 1972, pp. 95–96. Similar considerations, even if starting from different premises, are made by Ananda Kentish Coomaraswamy: 'East and West disagree on goals only because the West is *determined*, that is, decided and economically "resolved" to move towards an indefinite goal, and calls "progress" this moving adrift' (*Eastern Wisdom and Western Knowledge*, Italian edition; J. T. Fraser, *The Familiar Stranger*, Amherst MA, 1987. Italian translation, p. 224. Milan 1975, p. 94).

9 R. Rorty, *La filosofia dopo la filosofia*, with a preface by A.G. Gargani, Laterza, Rome-Bari 1989, p. 15.

10 I discussed more in depth the position of Vattimo and of 'weak thought' in my essay *'Idola' del postmoderno*, in *Filosofia '87*, Roma-Bari 1988, pp. 163ff.

11 I had already formulated this expression when I encountered a seemingly analogous one, *ontologie éclatée*, in the recent book by Pierre Caussat, *L'événement*, Paris 1992 (see ibid., pp. 175ff).

12 I think that, at least in this respect, we can agree with G. Jervis' position, *La psicoanalisi come esercizio critico*, Milan 1989, pp. 13ff.

13 E. Gellner, '*Tractatus Sociologico-Philosophicus*', in *Culture, Identity and Politics*, Cambridge 1987, p. 176.

Chapter 7

1 *Conf.* XI, 14.17.

2 P. Valéry, *Cahiers*, IV. Italian edition, *Quaderni*, Volume 4, translated by Ruggero Guarini, Adelphi, Milan 1990, p. 84.

3 See G. Marramao, *Potere e secolarizzazione*, Roma 1985.

4 On this aspect, even if in a phenomenological perspective of a Husserlian kind, see H. Blumenberg, *Lebenszeit und Weltzeit*, Frankfurt am Main 1986, particularly pp. 295ff.

5 On this theme, see J. Gimpel, *La fin de l'avenir*, Paris 1992.

6 I. Kant, *Anthropology from a Pragmatic Point of View* (1789). Italian edition, *Antropologia pragmatica*, translated by Giovanni Vidari, revised by Augusto Guerra, Laterza, Rome-Bari 1985, pp. 122–23.

7 This theoretical interest was the focus of my previous book, *Minima temporalia*, as aptly noted by U. Galimberti, *Idee: il catalogo è questo*, Milan 1992, *ad vocem* 'Tempo', pp. 272–75.

8 See H. Blumenberg, *Säkularisierung und Selbstbehauptung*, Frankfurt am Main 1974 (new and extended edition of the first two parts of *Die Legimität der Neuzeit*, Frankfurt am Main 1966).

9 See J. Habermas, *Philosophisch-politische Profile*, Frankfurt am Main 1981; *Der philosophische Diskurs der Moderne*, Frankfurt am Main 1985. Italian edition, *Il discorso filosofico della modernità*, translated by Emilio Agazzi and Elena Agazzi, Laterza, Rome-Bari 1991.

10 See S. Mazzarino, *L'intuizione del tempo nella storiografia classica*, in *Il pensiero storico classico*, II, 2, Bari 1966, pp. 412–461. For a discussion of this important essay, I must again refer to my *Potere e secolarizzazione* (n 3) pp. xxviff. On the passage of 'history' from the classical paradigm of autopsy and 'eye-witness' to the modern one of semiotic practice, see J. Lozano, *Il discorso storico*, with preface by U. Eco, Palermo 1991.

11 See P. Rossi, *Le similitudini, le analogie, le articolazioni della natura*, now in *I ragni e le formiche*, Bologna 1986, pp. 119–126. Rossi has recently come back on the theme of the intertwining of time's 'arrow' and 'cycle' (also based on the book by S. J. Gould, *Time's Arrow, Time's Cycle*, Cambridge, MA, 1987. Italian edition, *La freccia del tempo, il ciclo del tempo. Mito e metafora nella scoperta del tempo geologico*, translated by Libero Sosio, Feltrinelli, Milan 1989) and, as a consequence, also on the criticism of the 'linear' versions of secularization (see P. Rossi in *Il passato, la memoria, l'oblio*, Il Mulino, Bologna 1991).

12 Faced with the actual world setting, we could never sufficiently stress the testamentary value of the statements contained in the *Vorbemerkung* to the *Gesammelte Aufsätze zur Religionssoziologie*, written by Weber shortly before his death: 'The questions of universal history will inevitably and legitimately be treated, by the children of the modern European cultural world, based on this problematic formulation: what chain of events has made it possible that cultural phenomena, which – at least so we like to think – were developed in a universal line of meaning and validity, became manifest *precisely in the West, and only here*?' (*The Sociology of Religion*. Italian edition, *Sociologia della religione*, ed. and introduction by Pietro Rossi, Edizioni di Comunità, Milan 1982, p. 3). Those phenomena are immediately listed with lapidary clarity: '*Only in the West* there exists a "science" at that stage of development that we, today, recognize as "valid"'; '*Only in the West* there existed [. . .] a rational and systematic practice of science, and therefore the specialists trained for it'; 'No country and no era have ever witnessed, *in the sense that the modern West has*, the absolute and rigid framing of all our existence, of the fundamental political, technical and economic conditions of our lives, into the structure of an organization of officials trained in a specific way. [. . .] The 'State' itself, in the sense of a political institution with a rationally established 'Constitution', with a rationally established law and an administration consigned to specialized officials, according to rationally established rules, that is, 'laws', is *only characteristic of the West* – in this essential combination of fundamental elements, independently from all the other beginnings of the same kind that we can find elsewhere. [. . .] *Only thc West* charged similar laws and administration, with such technical-juridical and formalistic perfection, with the management of the economy' (Ibid., pp. 3–12). In all the peculiar cases mentioned above, we witness 'a specifically postured 'rationalism' of Western culture' (Ibid., pp. 12–13). Hence the command -and the weighty heritage - that Weber transmitted to us: 'It is again about [. . .], first of all, recognizing and explaining, in its origins, the particular *specific mode* of *Western rationalism* and, within this, of *modern* Western rationalism' (Ibid., p. 13). All emphases are added.

13 L. Spitzer, *L'armonia del mondo*, Il Mulino, Bologna 1967, p. 179 (originally published as *Classical and Christian Ideas of World Harmony*>, Baltimore 1963).

14 A. de Tocqueville, *De la démoctratie en Amérique* (1830), in N. Matteucci (ed.), *Scritti politici*, II, UTET, Turin 1968, p. 825.

15 For an analysis of the recent developments in the secularization debate, see my article 'Säkularisierung', in *Historisches Wörterbuch der Philosophie*, VIII, Schwabe Verlag, Basel 1992. The themes of this article then found a broader development in another book of mine: *Die Säkularisierung der westlichen Welt*, Insel Verlag, Frankfurt am Main 1996.

16 See Christopher Lasch, The *True and Only Heaven.* Italian edition. *Il Paradiso in terra. Il progresso e la sua critica*, translated by Carlo Oliva, Feltrinelli, Milan 1992, p. 39.

17 See R.A. Nisbet, *Social Change and History*. Italian edition, *Storia e cambiamento sociale*, translated by Stefano Magni, IBL, Milan 1977, particularly pp. 63ff. (devoted to the 'Augustinian metaphor'); *History of the Idea of Progress*, New York 1980, particularly pp. 297ff. (on the 'persistence of progress').

18 See Lasch (n 16).

19 Ibid., p. 41.

20 Ibid., p. 42.

21 See Marramao (n 3) pp. 41ff.

22 E. Gellner, '*Tractatus Sociologico-Philosophicus*', in *Culture, Identity and Politics*, Cambridge 1987, p. 179.

23 Ibid.

24 Ibid.

25 Ibid., p. 180.

26 Ibid., pp. 180–181.

27 Ibid., p. 180.

28 With this connotation, of the absolute contingency and freedom of individual choice from any form of heteronymous authority, the secularization theorem is adopted, today, by the most radical perspectives: from Peter L. Berger's 'heretical imperative' to the most recent developments in the bio-ethical debate. See, for example, H. Tristram Engelhardt Jr., *Bioethics and Secular Humanism. The Search for a Common Morality*, London and Philadelphia 1991, particularly pp. 20ff.

29 This meaningful expression is taken from M. Theunissen, *Negative Theologie der Zeit*, Franfurt am Main 1991.

30 See Moishe ben Maimoun, *Dalâlat al-'Hâyirîn*, II, 16: 'if we are led to absurd consequences when admitting creation, we are pushed towards an even greater absurdity when admitting eternity'. See also the text of the French edition: Maimonide, *Le Guide des Égarés*, edited by S. Munk, Paris 1981, v.2, p. 129. For a recent discussion on this aspect, I refer to the essay by Ze'ev Levy, 'Ultimate Reality and Meaning in Maimonides' Concept of God and Creation', in *Ultimate Reality and Meaning*', vol. XIV (1991), no. 3, pp. 165–174.

31 See G.W.F. Hegel, *Enciclopedia delle scienze filosofiche in compendio* (1830), Bari 1963, p. 217.

32 For this aspect, I refer to the contributions by F. Corrao, D. Meghnagi and L. Russo during the discussion on my book, *Minima temporalia*, organized and published (ed. G. Nebbiosi) by the journal *Koinos*. 'Gruppo e funzione analitica', XII (1991), 1, pp. 10–71.

33 On the 'Gnostic-hermetic' traces of Heidegger's *Seinsvergessenheit*, see U. Eco, *I limiti dell'interpretazione*, Milan 1990, p. 49; Rossi, *Il passato, la memoria, l'oblio* (n 11) pp. 16–18.

34 See V. Farias, *Heidegger and Nazism*. Italian edition, *Heidegger e il nazismo*, eds P. Amari and M. Marchetti, Bollati Boringhieri, Turin 1988.

35 M. Zarader, *La dette impensée. Heidegger et l'héritage hébraique*, Paris 1990: see, in particular, pp. 70ff. (on the 'double essence of thought' in Heidegger) and p. 92 (on 'memory' and 'denegation'). Based on the unconscious or removed Jewish traces underlying his thought, we could argue (as has been done, for example, by Derrida himself) that the reason of the *Ereignis* is at least virtually independent from the plot of the *Seinsgeschichte*, intended as the 'History of Meaning'. Such an argument faces, however, a further and theoretically more risqué difficulty: the *Ereignis* itself supports the idea (that is ultimately 'domesticating' and anthropocentric) of the reciprocal belonging between Man and being. So that, as clearly spelled out in the *Beiträge zur Philosophie, in Gesamtausgabe* (hereafter GA), LXV, Frankfurt am Main 1989, § 133: 'being needs Man in order to unfold', while 'Man belongs to being in order to fulfill his ultimate destination as *Da-sein*'.

36 H. Corbin, *Le paradoxe du Monothéisme*. Italian edition, *Il paradosso del monoteismo*, translated by G. Rebecchi, Marietti, Casale Monferrato 1986; esp. pp. 3–28 on the relation of *difference* between the 'God-one' and the 'multiple divinities'.

Chapter 8

1 M. Heidegger, *Die Grundprobleme der Phänomenologie*, GA XXIV, Frankfurt am Main 1975, p. 328. For an extended *Auseinandersetzung* with Bergson's *temps-durée*, see the course of the winter semester 1925–1926 (GA XXI, § 21).

2 Arist., *Phys.* IV, 19 b 1–2.

3 See, for example, I. Düring, *Aristotele*, Milan 1976, pp. 341ff.

4 *Phys.* IV, 219 b 4-9.

5 Ibid., 223 a 21–28.

6 See E. Husserl, *Zur Phänomenologie des inneren Zeitbewusstseins*, Husserliana X, Den Haag 1966, p. 3. Italian edition, *Per la fenomenologia della coscienza interna del tempo (1893–1917)*, ed. Alfredo Marini, Franco Angeli Milan 1985.

7 *Phys.* IV, 217 b 34-35.

8 Already in *Potere e secolarizzazione* I had taken this expression from R. Koselleck, *Vergangene Zukunft*, Frankfurt am Main 1979. Italian edition, *Futuro passato. Per una semantica dei tempi storici*, Genoa 1986, but sensibly changed its meaning compared to its original historical-hermeneutical 'tendency'.

9 L. Spitzer, *L'armonia del mondo*, Il Mulino Bologna 1967, p. 179 (originally published as: *Classical and Christian Ideas of World Harmony*, Baltimore 1963), pp. 42–43.

10 *Mus.* VI, 3.4.

11 Spitzer (n 9) p. 43.

12 *Conf.* XI, 27.36.

13 GA XXIV, p. 1.

14 M. Heidegger, *Der Begriff der Zeit* (1924), Tübingen 1989, pp. 19 and 21.

15 See Heidegger, *Die Grundprobleme der Phänomenologie* (n 1) p. 329.

16 It is a 'syndrome' that we find in Bergson himself: 'duration is the continual progress of the past that erodes the future and that grows while proceeding. And because it endlessly grows, the past is also indefinitely preserved' (*L'évolution créatrice*, Milan 1936, p. 12).

17 See *Phys.* IV, 222 b 16: *Metabolè de pasa physei ekstatikón*. Here, Aristotle refers to sudden change, which, by its nature, is able to have things spring from itself.

18 Heidegger (n 1) p. 378: 'Die ursprünglishe Zeit ist in sich selbst—das ist das Wesen ihrer Zeitigung—ausser sich. Sie ist dieses Ausser-sich selbst . . .'.

19 A very good example, in this sense, is in S. N. Eisenstadt, *Civiltà comparate*, Naples 1990.

20 The expression is taken from L. Kolakowski, *Metaphysical Horror*, Oxford 1988.

21 For a critical discussion of this work – whose materials, as we know, date back to the period 1936–1946 – see G. Marramao, *Minima temporalia. Tempo, spazio, esperienza*, Milano 1990, pp. 68ff.

22 Heidegger, (n 14) p. 27.

Chapter 9

1 See T. Gold, *La natura del tempo*, in G. Toraldo di Francia (ed.), *Il problema del cosmo*, Rome 1982.

2 I. Prigogine, *De l'être au devenir*. Italian edition, *Dall'essere al divenire*, Einaudi, Turin 1986, p. xii.

3 W.V.O. Quine, *Quidditates*, Milan 1991, pp. 224–226.

4 M. Heidegger, *Der Begriff der Zeit* (1924), Tübingen 1989, p. 7.

5 This is also at the root of the renewed interest in a connection between theology and science. See, for example, the collection of essays in R. J. Russell, W. R. Stoeger, G. V. Coyne (eds), *Physics, Philosophy and Theology*, Vatican City 1988.

6 To be precise, the expressions infinitely large/infinitely small should no longer be used, given that the contemporary cosmic (and cosmological) *disorientation* now consists in the correspondence between 'distance' and 'time', exploration of space and exploration of universe's past (with the ensuing possibility of observing the Big Bang, the Genesis, from our location in space).

7 Here is where my argument departs from A. Masullo's in *Filosofie del soggetto e diritto del senso*, Genoa 1990; on the other hand, I agree with the author's idea of the need of a philosophical development that is resolved neither into *apodixis*, nor into Heidegger's 'anti-theoretical' and 'de-constructionistic' reform. The following considerations, therefore, are also valid as a first-cut answer to the comments I received from Masullo himself in the abovementioned essay *Sulla questione del 'tempo'*.

8 See W.R. Bion, *Elements of Psycho-Analysis*. Italian edition, *Gli elementi della psicoanalisi*, translated by F. Hautmann, *Armando* editore, Rome 1979, p. 33.

9 F. Riolo, *Sogno e teoria della conoscenza in psicoanalisi*, in C. Neri, A. Correale, P. Fadda (eds), *Letture bioniane*, Rome 1987, p. 69.

10 W.R. Bion, *Learning from Experience*. Italian edition, *Apprendere dall'esperienza*, translated by Antonello Armando, Rome 1972, p. 45. In light of Bion's revision of the relationship between dreaming and unconsciousness, it would be necessary, at this point, to start a critical consideration of the limited (and ultimately secondary) role that *phantasia* and *imaginatio* play in Freud's work.

11 E. Benveniste, '*Latin tempus*', in *Mélanges Ernout*, Paris 1940, pp. 11–16.

12 'Almost' means, here, 'except for Michel Serres', the only one, to my knowledge, who understood the centrality of this aspect: 'By wisdom or chance the French language, like the Italian, uses one word to indicate both the time that passes and flows—*time, Zeit*—and the condition—*weather, Wetter*—produced by climate and by those that our forefathers used to call meteors' (*Le contrat naturel*. Italian edition, *Il contratto naturale*, translated by Alessandro Serra, Feltrinelli, Milan 1991, p. 41).

13 Benveniste, *Latin tempus* (n 11) p. 13. We should at least mention Harald Weinrich's important work, *Tempus. La funzione dei tempi nel testo*, Bologna 1978. The thread of this book moves from a linguistic to a literary analysis and, while comparatively examining the verbal forms in Latin and in the various Western European languages, argues that these, when structuring the temporal order of the narrative text, are not simple logical forms, but linguistic signs aimed at directing the receptive attitude of the reader.

14 For the fusion of the Greek *kairós* and the Latin *occasio* in the figure of Chance, we must refer to E. Panofsky, '*Il padre tempo*', in *Studi in iconologia*, Turin 1975, pp. 91–92.

15 The hypothesis of the possible derivation of *kairós* from the Indo-European root **krr-* had already been argued by E. Boisacq who, nevertheless, dealt with it in conjunction with the alternative relation of the term with *krisis* in the sense of *discrimen*, 'decision' (see P. Chantraine, *Dictionnaire étymologique de la langue grecque: histoire des mots*, I, Paris 1968, pp. 392–393). Similarly, H. Frisk, while mentioning Benveniste's argument, presents the hypothesis—based on Wilamowitz—of a derivation from *keiro*, with the ensuing meaning of 'decisive moment', *entscheidender Augenblick*, or 'time segment', *Zeitabschnitt* (see *Griechisches etymologisches Wörterbuch*, I, Heidelberg 1960, pp. 755–756). P. Chantraine, after recalling Beneveniste's hypothesis, advances other arguments: for example, that of a relationship with *krino* (still related to the Latin *discrimen*) or with *kyro* that would render, 'despite the phonetic difficulty, the idea of intersection' (see P. Chantraine, *Dictionnaire étymologique de la langue grecque*, II, Paris 1970, p. 480b). The association of *kairós* with *tempestivitas* and with *tempus opportunum*, instead, can be found in *Thesaurus Graecae Linguae*, ab Henrico Stephano constructus, IV, Oarisiis 1841, cc. 817–818.

As for Latin etymological dictionaries, we should mention the distance between Benveniste's position and that held by Ernout and Meillet, for whom tempus would designate the 'fraction de la durée', as opposed to *aevus*, *aevum*, which would indicate 'le temps dans sa continuité' (see A. Ernout-A. Meillet, *Dictionnaire étymologique de la langue latine. Histoire des mots*, Paris 1932, p. 982). A. Walde and J.B. Hoffmann, who comment on Benveniste's essay, advance the hypothesis of a gradual evolution of *tempus* from *tempestas/keránnymi* towards *chronos* (see *Lateinisches etymologisches Wörterbuch*, II, Heidelberg 1954^3, pp. 660–661). For the purposes of a cultural clarification, besides the historical-terminological one, it is useful to recall that the first definition of 'Middle Ages' is that of *media tempestas* (see the article 'Modern', written by H.U. Gumbrecht for the *Geschichtliche Grundbegriffe. Historisches Lexikon zur politisch-sozialen Sprache in Deutschland*, IV, Stuttgart 1978, p. 98). It is also unusual that some Italian etymological dictionaries, while arguing for the derivation of *tempestas* from the adjective *tempestus* (= 'tempestivo') and connotating it also with the meaning of 'age', or 'season', insist on the conclusion that the etymology of the word 'time' is still uncertain (see, for example, C. Battisti-G. Alessio, *Dizionario etimologico italiano*, V, Florence 1975, pp. 3746–3747).

16 On this, see S. Natoli, '*Telos, skopós, éschaton. Tre figure della storicità*', in *Teatro filosofico*, Milan 1991, p. 33.

17 Plato's notion of *kairós*, as contained in *Resp*. II, 370b-c, seems close to this meaning. In this passage, Plato speaks of the 'appropriate time', ignoring which the craftsman's work breaks down. For obvious reasons, I must ignore here the theological developments of *kairós* that, starting with the New Testament writings, acquires a meaning close to *éschaton*. On this point, refer to the first part of my book *Potere e secolarizzazione*.

18 C. Schmitt, *Raum und Rom. Zur Phonetik des Wortes Raum*, in 'Universitas', VI (1951), No. 9, p. 966. For an insightful analysis of this essay, see G. Raciti, *Dello spazio*, with afterword by M. Sgalambro, Catania 1990, pp. 59ff. Incidentally, we should recall that the etymological derivation of *spatium* from *pateo* is scrutinized in Ernout-Meillet (see p. 703); while in Walde-Hoffmann, even if this hypothesis is not discarded, the stress is put on the derivation of the term from the Indo-European roots **spe-, *spa-*, as well as on its original meaning as 'space for walking': hence the German words *Spazieren, Spaziergang, Spazierweg* (see pp. 568–569).

19 In particular, I am thinking here of the *thema mundi* of Wallace Stevens' 'poem' (even if it is much more than poetry). Here Being is indeed Time, but in the sense of weather: 'Weather by Franz Hals,/ Brushed up by brushy winds in brushy clouds,/ Wetted by blue, colder for white' (*Notes toward a Supreme Fiction: It Must be Abstract*, VI). I thank Nadia Fusini for bringing this to my attention. In fact, we all owe to her the excellent care and the translation and introduction (that are simply fabulous) of the Italian edition of these texts by Stevens: *Note verso la finzione suprema*, Venice 1987).

20 In this respect, Einstein's letter to Born (4 December 1926) is telling: 'Quantum mechanics deserves all our respect, but an *inner voice* tells me that it is not yet the right solution. It is a theory that tells us much, but does not allow us to penetrate further the secret of the Great Old Man. In any case, I am convinced that *he* does not play dice with the world' (A. Einstein and M. Born, *The Born–Einstein Letters: Friendship, Politics and Physics in Uncertain Times*, with foreword by B. Russell and introduction by W. Heisenberg, (Italian edition, *Scienza e vita. Lettere 1916–1955*), Turin 1973, pp. 108–109).

21 P. Valéry, *Cahiers*, IV. Italian edition, *Quaderni*, Vol. 4, Adelphi, Milan 1990, p. 454.

22 See E. Levinas, *Time and the Other*. Italian edition, *Il Tempo e l'Altro*, ed. Francesco Paolo Ciglia, Il Melangolo, Genoa 1987, p. 51. On this point, see also Marco M. Olivetti's considerations on the 'pause of being' (*Analogia del soggetto*, Rome-Bari 1992, esp. pp. 167ff).

23 Stated otherwise, the century that is about to end has *not* been the 'century of philosophy'.

INDEX

Note: 'n' indicates an endnote, with the number following 'n' indicating the endnote number.